Improving Your Storytelling

Improving Your Storytelling

Beyond the Basics
for All Who Tell Stories
in Work or Play

Doug Lipman

August House Publishers, Inc.
ATLANTA

To my mother,
who always made me feel wanted,
didn't care what the neighbors thought,
and taught me to enjoy thunderstorms.

©1999 by Doug Lipman.
All rights reserved. This book, or parts thereof, may not be
reproduced or publicly presented, in any form without permission.
Published 1999 by August House, Inc.,
3500 Piedmont Road, Suite 310 Atlanta, GA 30305, 404-442-4420
www.augusthouse.com
Printed in the United States of America

10 9 8 7

LIBRARY OF CONGRESS CATALOGING-IN-PUBLICATION DATA
Lipman, Doug.
Improving your storytelling : beyond the basics
for all who tell stories in work or play / Doug Lipman.
p.   cm.
Includes bibliographical references (p.) and index.
ISBN-13: 978-0-87483-530-4 (alk. paper)
ISBN-10: 0-87483-530-5 (alk. paper)
1. Storytelling. 2. Public speaking. I. Title.
PN4193.I5L56   1999   99-26088
808.5'43—dc21   CIP

Executive editor: Liz Parkhurst
Project editors: Jason H. Maynard, Joy Freeman
Copyeditor: Tom Baskett, Jr.
Book design and illustration: Joy Freeman
Cover design: Desktop Miracles

AUGUST HOUSE, INC.   PUBLISHERS   ATLANTA

CONTENTS

ACKNOWLEDGMENTS

This book has grown over my whole life as a storyteller and coach. That means I have many people to thank.

Who did I learn all this from? The children who were my first listeners—starting with my brother, Brad, who first taught me the value of a loving listener. My parents, Paul and Virginia Lipman, who were delighted to listen to both of us. I learned also from my classmates. My good teachers. My friends. My students. Storytellers I have coached. My colleagues.

I took my own recommendation and asked for lots of help with this book. Jay O'Callahan read much of the manuscript, helped me clarify and appreciate my own thinking, and consistently championed the value of this book. Linda Palmström, Christine Shumock, Fran Yardley, and Marsha Saxton gave specific suggestions and, even more importantly, listened to me think aloud. Karen De Mauro drew on her vast expertise to make helpful suggestions on the chapter on kinesthetic imagery. Glenn Morrow, heroic editor of *The Museletter,* interviewed me sensitively; some of the thoughts I first expressed there have been re-expressed here.

Pam McGrath read the entire manuscript and became the midwife of the final revisions. She listened to me on long phone calls as I rethought the structure of the conclusion, wrestled with thorny rewriting, and thought aloud about new examples to make the concepts clear. In the end, she was brilliant enough to suggest a dozen examples from her own experience of other storytellers and generous enough to allow me to use them.

Some people took the time to read the first draft of this manuscript and give comments. Their careful help has made a big difference. Laura Gold's comments were highly encouraging. Diane MacInnes, Carrie van der Laan, and Laura Beasley wrote their suggestions; Theo Beasley Henderson passed his along through Laura.

I did the actual writing in the company of my devoted crew of "writing buddies," especially Marsha Saxton and Linda Langford. Other writing companions were Terry Marotta and Robbie Tovey.

Where did I write? I wrote almost every word in a splendid writers' environment, the Brookline Deli. Always ready to joke when I wanted a diversion, to cook when I wanted food, and to leave me undisturbed for the long hours when I wanted to write, Michael, Michael, and Jeff are the godparents of this manuscript. I will miss them all, even as I write happily under the approving eyes of the new owners.

Some portions of this book appeared, in earlier versions, in *The National Storytelling Journal, Storytelling Magazine,* and *Storytelling World.* I thank all the editors who encouraged me to write for them and who gave my work a place in their crowded pages.

Liz and Ted Parkhurst, the owners of August House, deserve thanks not only from me, but from all who care about storytelling. They have had the vision and the commitment to make available an impressive catalog of storytelling resources.

INTRODUCTION: STORYTELLING BASICS AND BEYOND

In the last decades, storytelling has been discovered as an art form and a professional tool. People are now performing stories in theaters and on radio and television, as well as for business luncheons, libraries, schools, and religious organizations. Others are using storytelling as a tool in their various kinds of work—as therapists, teachers, community organizers, lawyers, health-care workers, sales personnel, public speakers, business managers.

The first steps in storytelling are often easy. After all, everyone tells stories in everyday life. Whether you think of yourself as a "storyteller" or not, you tell people what happened to you.

Once you take storytelling into the more formal contexts of performance and occupational uses, however, you may find yourself with problems to solve and questions to ask. You may find yourself trying to get a handle on the structure of an unwieldy story, or struggling with performance anxiety. You may find it difficult to learn new stories, or to keep the old ones alive and interesting. You may be wondering why your audience gets so quiet when you tell a particular tale, or pondering the question, "How can I remember the character voices I develop?"

You need information that goes beyond the basics of storytelling. And you need it in a form that does not just tell you what to do, but helps you to make your own informed decisions.

This book is meant for the reader who has already told some stories and is ready to learn more about storytelling. It gives you the things to consider when making your own decisions—but leaves it to you to judge the pros and cons of your particular situation. Instead of advice or rules to follow, it gives you a series of frameworks that will encourage you to think for yourself.

Fundamentally, you need to be present. Whether it is a piece of gossip told to a neighbor across the fence or a two-hour theatrical story performed at Lincoln Center, storytelling always constitutes an *event*. A story can only be told at a particular place and time, with someone telling it and someone else listening.

Not every art form requires the artist's active presence. You may paint a painting in one long day in the white heat of inspiration. Or you may paint in five-minute intervals spread over months or years. But once the painting is done, it is done. The need for you to balance all the elements of your painting—to create patterns of color, shape, and texture—is over. A painting can exist and be enjoyed even when the painter is absent.

When you tell a story, however, you must always be there, shaping the artistic moment. Even if you have told a story five hundred times before, you must still show up the five hundred and first time, balancing the demands of the story, your needs, and the needs of the audience.

Being there requires a physical presence, of course, but it also calls for your intellectual, emotional, and imaginative presence. It implies that you actively coordinate all the artistic and practical elements in the storytelling event. In short, being present means thinking in the present as you tell.

Thinking in the Present

I use the term "thinking in the present" to include not just conscious, analytical thought, but also unconscious, intuitive, nonlinear forms of thinking. It describes a complete process that begins with your taking in all the relevant information (about the story, yourself, your listeners, and the context in which you are telling) as well as your responses (including the story you tell, how you tell it, and your remarks and actions before and after).

Actually, your thinking is even more complex than that. As you tell your story, you continue to receive new information about the audience and even new realizations about the story. You then integrate both into your telling. You continue to think: to notice, to integrate, and to change your responses to the situation.

Like a sailboat skipper reacting to local conditions, a good storyteller responds to constantly changing influences: the context of the storytelling event, the audience, the story, and the storyteller's own needs and abilities.

HELPING YOU MAKE YOUR OWN DECISIONS

Imagine you are a student painter. If you bring a painting to an expert artist for help, the expert may be able to change the painting in a way that makes it more effective. If the expert adds a blob of red paint in the upper right-hand corner, it stays there.

But if an expert tries to improve your storytelling, he or she will not always be there when the story is told. The expert cannot take into account all the changes that a story will go through in the course of a particular storytelling event. It's as though your painting turns into a video screen that keeps changing, but the blob of red paint remains on the outside of the screen. The red blob may have improved the appearance at one moment, but it may seriously interfere when the picture changes.

Thus, the best assistance doesn't "fix" your story or tell you what to do. The best help improves your ability to make your own decisions. It doesn't paint the screen; it helps you learn how to change the image on the screen to meet the constantly changing demands of the moment.

THE CASE OF THE (POSSIBLY) BAD SECOND PERFORMANCE

From time to time, I will hear a storyteller say, "But I want to know how to fix my story once and for all!"

This desire, though common and understandable, contains within it the seeds of failure.

Most of us experience a strong pull to stop thinking in the present. We say to ourselves, "Now I have finally learned how to tell to a preschool audience; at last, that learning is completed." Or we say,

"I worked hard learning my story, and now I want to just take it easy." Or we see someone performing effortlessly and imagine that they are coasting—rather than thinking with such great efficiency that no effort shows.

Great performance does not necessarily require great effort. But the moment we stop thinking in the present, we begin to fail.

Take the case of the Bad Second Performance. One day, you tell a story successfully. You know in your bones that something wonderful happened, and that you had a big part in it. You think, "Ah! Now I know how to tell that story!"

What happens the next time you tell the story? If you keep your focus on replicating your previous success, it usually bombs!

Why did it fail the second time? Because you were not thinking about the current situation. You were thinking about the previous performance, when it succeeded so brilliantly. As a result, your attention was not where it had been during the successful telling— on creatively balancing all the needs of the moment. You stopped thinking in the present, and your storytelling suffered.

NOT ADVICE BUT UNDERSTANDING

Now you can see why advice is often unhelpful. It makes you think things like, "I should never change a folktale. I should stop saying, 'Um.' I should try to make eye contact." These thoughts tend to take you out of the moment, diverting your attention from what is actually happening during the storytelling event.

In this sense, all advice is bad advice. The thought "I should look my listeners in the eye" may distract you just as much as "I should *not* look my listeners in the eye."

What *is* helpful? It is useful to have information and principles that can help you make decisions in the moment of telling a story (or in your preparation). You need to know the effects and trade-offs involved in various decisions you might make. You need ways of thinking about your storytelling that will strengthen your effectiveness as a decision maker. Other people's experiences (their stories about their storytelling) can be invaluable in learning about these principles and ways of thinking—as long as they are not viewed as examples to be rigidly imitated or rigidly avoided.

No Right Way to Tell Stories

Since each situation is unique, it follows that there is no one right way to tell stories. There is only a way that works for *you* at a given moment with a given audience. Thus, the storyteller's job is not to imitate "the perfect storyteller" or "ideal storytelling." It is to find a way to tell that meets the requirements of the moment—which may never again repeat.

LOCALLY PREFERRED STYLES

Local communities of storytellers often develop a preferred style of storytelling—which may become confused with "the right way to tell stories." This community may consist of a group of friends who tell stories informally at social occasions. Alternatively, it may include traditional storytellers in a family or ethnic group. Then again, it may comprise a peer group of occupational storytellers in a corporation or industry. Or it may consist of a regional association of free-lance professional performers.

Any such community may prefer stories told in a particular style—dramatic, conversational, solemn and didactic, or with multimedia props. Such a style may have derived from the influence of a few pioneering storytellers in the community. In a traditional or tradition-inspired community, it may also derive from generations of accepted practice.

In religious, educational, or occupational communities, a preferred style may even derive from a particular application of a philosophy of storytelling. Some professional librarians, for example, believe that storytelling in a library is purely a means to encourage reading, and therefore should be done with as few nonverbal forms of expression as possible.

If a community has such a "preferred style" of storytelling, this style forms part of the expectations for any storytelling event within the community. If you violate a community's expectations by telling in a different style, you will get a corresponding response from your listeners—whether of puzzlement, disapproval, or delight. Your listeners may even couch their disapproval in categorical terms: "That wasn't really storytelling," or "Good storytelling always incorporates other art forms."

No matter how moralistic someone's disapproval may sound, however, storytelling style is not a matter of absolutes. Any particular style will be likely to succeed in an appropriate set of circumstances. Instead of worrying whether a particular style is "right," "good," or "proper," we can focus on finding a way to make each unique storytelling event successful for all involved.

STYLE VERSUS EFFECTIVENESS

From time to time, beginning storytellers have approached me in a panic, saying, "So-and-so said that storytellers shouldn't tell a story word-for-word (or: change the author's words...use props or musical instruments...stand up while telling...sit down while telling...use accents..., etc.) But I do that!"

I usually reply like this: "Michael Parent juggles. When he started to tell stories, it was natural for him to use juggling to get his stories across. I sing and play instruments. When I try to tell a story, it is often natural for me to use music to help. Does that mean that you should juggle or play the button accordion? No! It means that you should do whatever seems natural *to you* to get your story across. That may include sitting quietly on your hands, or doing something that no storyteller has ever done before. Don't try to be right, try to be yourself!"

I have seen storytellers like Alice Kane of Ontario, Canada, who tells stories without props of any kind. In fact, she doesn't even use hand gestures. To maximize our focus on her words, she rarely even uses facial expression—except for the occasional, sly half-wink. She is a great storyteller. When the story begins, she comes afire with her tone of voice, with rhythm, with the images and feelings in her stories, with her fascination with words—and with her desire to share her delight. I could listen to her for twenty-four hours straight, and be entranced the whole time.

At the same time, I have seen great storytellers who dance across the stage, use magic tricks, or wear costumes. Their style is their own decision; I only care if they communicate effectively to me. Style and effectiveness are independent of each other. If you find your individual way of communicating what you love, your style will find you.

My storytelling style will derive from a balanced mix of what comes naturally for me, what I want to convey, and what works for my audience. Effectiveness consists of finding a workable harmony among all the components of the storytelling event.

The Storytelling Triangle

To understand the storytelling event, look at its major components. One is the transfer of imagery that occurs, and its building blocks: oral language and images. A second, not dealt with in this book, is the *context* of the event, the physical and social setting in which a story is told. Finally, there are three obvious ingredients: the storyteller, the audience, and the story. These three form the corners of a triangle—the storytelling triangle.

How do the corners of the storytelling triangle relate to each other? First, the storyteller has a relationship with the audience. This relationship might be decades old, or just formed as the story is begun. Second, the storyteller has a relationship with the story. This includes intellectual understanding of the story, emotional experience of the story, and the memory or imagining of the story. These first two relationships are represented by the solid lines in figure 1.

Although the first two relationships involve the storyteller directly, the third relationship (represented by a dotted line in figure 1) does not. In a successful storytelling event, the *audience* will form a positive relationship (a connection) with the *story*. As a storyteller, you can create one relationship with the story and another with the audience, but you are powerless to force the audience to create a relationship with the story. You can try to influence that third relationship through the relationships that involve you directly, but you can only prepare, suggest, offer, and then hope.

LOVING THE MYSTERY

Now you can see another important characteristic of storytelling: not only is telling an event in which the storyteller must keep thinking in the present, but a key goal (having the audience form a positive relationship with the story) is beyond the teller's direct control. To succeed at storytelling, then, you need to accept your inability to create this relationship directly. You need humility.

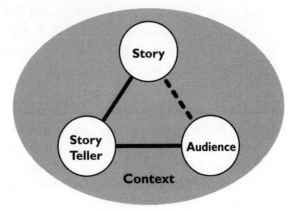

Figure 1: The Storytelling Triangle. The storyteller has no direct control over the audience's relationship to the story.

At the same time, you need to make effective use of the tools available to you to foster this relationship. You need persistence, clarity, ingenuity, and caring. In this regard, the storyteller resembles a gardener. You can plant the seeds, and provide the water and access to sunlight that they require. But you can never force the seeds to grow.

You must accept your inability to force the seeds to grow or to force the audience to respond to the story. But when the plant sprouts or the audience takes the story to their hearts, you can rejoice in the mystery of the process you have nurtured. The circumstance that forces you to be humble is also what makes it so miraculous when you succeed.

EXPLORING EACH COMPONENT

This book is organized according to the components of the storytelling event. The first section explores a key process in storytelling: the transfer of mental imagery through oral language. The next three discuss your relationships with each feature of the storytelling triangle: the story, your audience, and your self. The final section puts the components back together. When you tell a story effectively, your attention moves flexibly from one component to another—and creates a dynamic balance between the flesh of story performance and the living spirit of artistic transformation.

The Transfer
of Imagery

What actually takes place when a story is told? In the broadest sense, there is a transfer of imagery. Before the story is told, you—the storyteller—have mental images of the story. You see, hear, or feel the events of the story you are about to tell. After the story is told, the listeners have created their own mental images of the story. They see, hear, or feel the events of the story, too—but not necessarily in exactly the same way you did.

What happens to make *your* images cause *their* images? In storytelling, the bridge between your images and theirs is oral language—namely, the spoken word and its partners gesture, posture, facial expression, tone of voice, etc. (figure 2).

The basic ingredients of the transfer of imagery through story-

Figure 2: Oral Language, the bridge between the images

telling are oral language (chapter 1) and mental imagery (chapters 2, 3, and 4).

1
ORAL LANGUAGE

Stories use the medium of oral language. To be a truly effective storyteller, you need to capitalize on oral language's strengths—and compensate for its weaknesses.

Many storytellers are less effective than they could be, simply because they try to apply written-language concepts to the oral language of storytelling. This chapter contrasts oral and written language—not to demean written language (one of the great achievements of human civilization), but to provide concepts that highlight the nature of *oral* language. (And much of this applies to manual languages, such as American Sign Language.)

Look at the written language in this book. What elements does it use to convey meaning? First, it uses the letters that form words. Second, it uses punctuation. Third, it uses various typographical devices, such as typefaces, font sizes, italics, indentations, etc. Fourth, it uses pictures—graphical elements such as diagrams. Fifth, it communicates through the materials of the book itself: the size, thickness, color, and other qualities of the paper and the binding.

All the magic of writing is conveyed with those five kinds of elements. All the passion, logic, impetuousness, inevitability, and humor of written language is shaped, like sculpture, from the simple clay of words, punctuation, typography, pictures, and materials.

What about oral language? The only element it has in common with written language is words.

But oral language has many additional elements, such as tone of voice, gestures, posture, facial expression, eye behaviors, and several other forms of expression.

My schooling focused exclusively on written language.

Inadvertently, it left me feeling that only written language was "real" language. It ignored the rich complexities of the language I had used even before I entered kindergarten. My schooling not only neglected oral language; it encouraged me to overlook it as something potentially worthy of attention and capable of improvement.

Written language is, of course, invaluable. Nothing I have learned about oral language takes away from the value of the written word.

But since becoming a storyteller, I have also discovered the workings of oral language. I have learned that the elements of oral language allow different kinds of expression—and place different demands on me—than those of written language. Knowing the nature of oral language is, for a storyteller, like knowing the exact nature of paint for a portrait artist. To be sure, our knowledge of oral language is mostly unconscious, but our print orientation can make us ignore what we actually know how to do.

Oral language offers many elements that can communicate a given meaning. Also, it can simultaneously communicate more than one meaning. And time passes during an oral story in a strict way that is foreign to the reading experience. I call these qualities the variety of expression, the multidimensionality, and the time-based nature of oral language. These qualities underlie the unique expressiveness available to the storyteller.

The Variety of Expression

Oral language uses only one element of written language: words. All too often, oral language is unconsciously taken to consist of words and little else. This causes us to neglect the expressive possibilities of its varied elements, which form the building blocks of how stories are told.

The key expressive tools of oral language include tone of voice, facial expression, gestures, posture, eye behaviors, and orientation in space. They each allow the storyteller to convey meanings that, in written language, might need to be expressed primarily in words.

TONE OF VOICE

By "tone of voice" I mean a combination of vocal timbre, inflection, loudness, and perhaps other aural properties of a spoken voice. Taken together, they convey much of the meaning of the spoken word.

Imagine overhearing a conversation between two people in the next room. You can hear the voices, but can't really make out the words. What do you understand? Just from their tones of voice, you probably understand a lot about how both people are feeling. You may also know a lot about their relationship. For example, is one of them expecting the other to behave differently? Is one trying to wheedle something from the other? Is one guarded, while the other is trying to put the first at ease?

Here's an exercise. Alone or with a partner, you might experiment with showing intention through tone of voice. Decide what you want from your partner (or from an imagined other person), then try to express it through tone of voice alone, without meaningful words. Use "blah, blah, blah," repeat a single word you like ("umbrella, umbrella, umbrella"), or make up gibberish as you go. When you are done, it might be instructive to hear your partner's perception of what you wanted.

In the case of the conversation overheard in the next room, there may be a whole story told through tone of voice. From the changes in the speakers' tones of voice, you probably know the shape of their conversation. Did it start tentatively, proceed to eager sharing, and end with hope? Or did it begin casually but turn heated, only to end icily?

As an experiment, you might try telling a story that has no words. Try to "tell your story" only through changes of tone of voice. With what tone of voice will you start? End?

Tone of voice communicates to unborn babies. Much of the time, it also communicates across cultures—even across species.

With a partner (and an audience, if you like) you can play a theater game known as Gibberish. One person acts as the Storyteller, the other as the Translator. Without any planning, the Storyteller tells a story, one "sentence" at a time, in gibberish (the more expressive the tone of voice, the better). The Translator, who has no idea what the storyteller is talking about, creates an impromptu "translation" into English (or whatever language the audience speaks). The fun comes, first, from comparing and contrasting the tones of voice (and other oral language elements such as facial expression and posture) of the two players, and, second, from comparing and contrasting the tone of voice of the Storyteller with the words of the Translator.

Tone of voice is so strong that whenever it conflicts with word meanings, it always prevails. This primacy of tone over words makes sarcasm possible. It is also what makes it unsatisfying when a loved one says, "I will always love you" with a hesitant tone. It is what makes it fun to say to your dog in a loving tone of voice, "You are the most worthless bag of fleas in the whole world!" and watch her wag her tail as though receiving the highest praise.

Try the classic acting exercise of saying a single word with different tones of voice. For example, say the word "yes" joyfully. Then try it sadly, resignedly, seductively, hesitantly, or nervously. Try saying "yes" in a way that means "maybe"—or in a way that means "no."

Tone of voice conveys a wide spectrum of meanings. Part of the reason that we use a more limited vocabulary when talking than when writing is that we don't *need* as many words. Instead, we use tone of voice (and other elements of oral language) to distinguish the more specific meanings.

When my storytelling falters, my first thought is often, "Did I use the wrong words?" Since tone of voice is even more meaningful, I might better ask, "Did I use the wrong tone of voice?" For example, I coached an experienced storyteller who was new to middle-school audiences. She tried many new stories, only to be greeted with indifference by her pre-adolescent listeners. As soon as I heard her perform, I understood her problem. She was using a tone of voice that suggested condescension. Although her preschool audiences had tolerated her tone well, these older children could not hear beyond it to appreciate the meanings carried by her well-chosen words.

FACIAL EXPRESSION, GESTURES, AND POSTURE

Three effective carriers of meaning involve the expressive motions of our face, limbs, and torso, respectively. As the arts of dance and mime prove, they can carry a world of meanings.

Jackie Torrence is proof of the expressive power of facial expressions. She does not walk around or use large movements of her limbs. But she puts the same amount of expressiveness into the changing expressions on her face that other tellers would put into their whole bodies. As a result, we scarcely notice that she sits down as she tells. Her face does the dancing.

Gesture can carry great meaning, too. Jay O'Callahan tells an hour-long story about Richard Wheeler's 1500-mile kayak journey, "The Spirit of the Great Auk." Sitting in a chair, he paddles with an imaginary kayak paddle as he tells Richard's story. When he narrates Richard's memories or forays onto the land, he stops the paddling gesture. Whenever Richard returns to the kayak, Jay begins the gesture again. The tension in Jay's arms increases as the paddling becomes more difficult or when Wheeler is upset. This rhythmic gesture runs through the entire story like a thread, connecting the entire tale and orienting us silently but unmistakably to Wheeler's moods as well as his entries and exits from the kayak.

The tools of facial expression, gestures, and posture influence each other. A smiling facial expression, for example, when combined with a proud posture may communicate welcoming and happiness. The same smiling expression combined with a slouching posture, however, may communicate a submissive desire to please.

Similarly, these three tools change the meanings of spoken words. "I welcome you" (even if said with a truly inviting tone of voice) seems less like a genuine offer when spoken with a closed posture (arms folded, shoulders forward) than with an open posture of invitation.

Many unspoken cultural norms regulate the use of these tools of oral expression. Because we are usually unaware of both the norms and the tools, we make unconscious judgments of people based on their "body language." In a situation where large gestures are tolerated and even expected (for example, in a Southern Italian family or on the stage of a theater), the person who "sits on his hands" as he talks may be perceived as shy, weak, or unexpressive. In a situation where large gestures are unaccustomed or frowned on (e.g., a formal dinner at Buckingham Palace or a television talk show on a public broadcasting station in the United States), the person who "gesticulates wildly" may be seen as rude, aggressive, or "unbalanced."

Some gestures or facial expressions have widely understood

meanings in only one group of cultures, regardless of the language spoken. For example, some African-derived cultures regard "sucking your teeth" as an expression of insolence, whereas other cultures take it to be a sign of hesitancy—or else a personal idiosyncrasy with little communicative content.

In different situations, the same gesture will have different meanings. But in all circumstances, we rely on people's facial expression, gestures, and posture for important information about their intention and their emotional attitude toward us and toward what they are saying. As storytellers, we can use these silent elements of oral language to make clear, efficient statements of our intention toward the audience and of our characters' intentions toward each other.

EYE BEHAVIOR

The direction of our gaze communicates many things. Looking into our listener's eyes, for instance, suggests paying close attention to our listener—which may be welcome or not, depending on the culture and circumstances.

Storyteller Pam McGrath has learned to use eye contact to underline humor:

> I say something funny and get a small laugh. Then I pause and make prolonged, smiling eye contact with an individual, as if to say, 'Did you get that?' At that point, everyone laughs again, usually louder than before. The first time, they laughed at my joke. The second time, the audience and I were buddies, laughing together at what the storyteller just did.

Looking up and to one side as we pause in our speech usually suggests that we are searching our memory or thoughts in preparation for speaking. Looking straight down as we speak suggests submission, embarrassment, or absorption in our private thoughts or feelings. Our listeners understand (unconsciously) what these eye movements mean, and even expect us to alternate among them. To the extent that eye movements show we are imagining the events and images of our story, they often help our listeners do the same— even helping them picture the exact size or location of what we are describing. Individual cultures also develop "eye gestures" with particular meanings—such as "rolling the eyes" to indicate impatience or incredulity.

In general, most people use eye behaviors unconsciously, and with great flexibility and effectiveness. It is possible, I believe, to learn to use eye behavior consciously—but it is very difficult and seldom worth the effort. Most people who attempt to use eye behavior consciously only succeed in conveying a sense of stiffness or insincerity. They fall afoul of the variety of expression of oral language, which implies that oral language is too complex to be easily faked. While you focus on counterfeiting one element of oral language, another unconsciously gives you away.

Usually, the most effective way to "use" eye behaviors is to forget about them. Instead, focus on your relationship to your audience and what you want to share or communicate with them. Then give yourself permission to use whatever eye behaviors seem to carry your storytelling forward. This will free you to make eye contact at some moments and avert your eyes at others—as appropriate to what you are saying and to whom you are saying it.

A caution. This unselfconscious approach may fail when there are obstacles preventing your flexible use of eye movements—or when you and your listeners have different expectations about the meaning of eye contact.

One such obstacle is fear. People who are afraid or humiliated tend to avert their eyes—or to make aggressive eye contact in self-defense. If you are feeling afraid in a situation where you are not actually in danger, it is usually more helpful to deal directly with the fear than to attempt to change your eye behaviors. The common directions given by instructors to anxious storytellers (such as "Make eye contact at least three times with everyone in the room!" or "Look at a spot twelve inches over your listeners' heads!") usually just compound the problem. Instead of scared storytellers averting their eyes, you end up with scared storytellers making unsatisfying, mechanical "contact" in a way that further confuses the audience.

Other obstacles involve mismatched expectations between storyteller and listeners. What is considered "appropriate" eye contact depends in part on the social status of speaker and listener. For example, a young adult in many cultures would avert eyes from a respected elder, but make sustained eye contact with a child. As a result, any misunderstanding about the social standing of your audience may lead you to eye behavior that they consider puzzling or inappropriate.

Similar misunderstandings occur between people of different cultural backgrounds. In many African cultures (and much of African-American culture) the speaker is expected to look into the eyes of the listener, while the listener is expected to look down. In some Native American cultures, on the other hand, the speaker is the one who is expected to look away. In other cultures, such as that of the Maori of New Zealand, both speaker and listener are expected to avert eyes. And in most Northern European-derived cultures, speaker and listener are expected to sustain eye contact for a culturally specified length of time. In each of these groups, the same behavior (looking at the eyes of the other) sends a very different message. What is a sign of respect in one culture may be a sign of disrespect in another.

In these cases, just doing "what comes naturally" is not likely to be effective. Instead, it may help to view eye behavior (as well as bodily orientation, distance from your listener, and many other elements of oral expression) as part of the vocabulary of a new language, with which you must experiment cautiously but determinedly.

ORIENTATION IN SPACE

One of the most concrete elements of oral language is the storyteller's spatial relationship to the listeners. Our position relative to our listeners conveys meaning about our relationship and intentions. Saying "hello" from across the room is different from saying it nose-to-nose. Moving away as we speak suggests "distancing" (we use that term as a physical metaphor to describe the emotional reality), whereas moving closer may suggest focus, intimacy, or menace.

In almost every culture, speaking from above suggests authority; from below, submission. (Hence the judge's bench, the preacher's pulpit, and the kneeling of the supplicant.) Even at the same level, facing toward someone as we speak gives a different meaning from that given by turning our backs or facing to the side.

For storytellers, orientation in space is a primary tool—like eye behavior—in relating to our listeners. It can also be used as a dramatic tool to suggest the relationship between a character and the objects or people with which the character interacts.

Facing our listeners directly, for example, is a typical way that we let them know we are speaking to them, and facing away can show that we are momentarily off duty (as when we take a sip of water). Combined with other cues, it can also suggest that a character is speaking or is feeling lost, determined, or disgusted. In dialogue, the exact direction we face can show how a conversation passes from one character to another. Similarly, changing our height or distance from our listeners can serve to intensify or relax the impact of what we say.

I'll never forget my reaction the first time I saw Jay O'Callahan perform a Japanese folk tale, "Hiro the Gambler." I perceived the conversation between the small but cheeky gambler and the enormous god as occurring between two characters of vastly different heights. In retrospect, I was sure that Jay must have portrayed the god by standing on a chair and the gambler by kneeling on the floor. Then I saw the story again. To my amazement, Jay remained standing at stage level throughout the story. But when Hiro spoke to the god, he looked almost straight up. Answering, the god looked almost straight down. Jay had used this element of oral language to create a vivid image of different-sized characters.

Multidimensionality

The variety of expressive elements of oral language gives us a wealth of ways to convey any particular idea or feeling. The complexity of oral language goes beyond this variety, however, because several of these expressive elements can be used at once.

Oral language can simultaneously present a word, a tone of voice, a facial expression, a gesture, a posture, an eye direction, and an orientation in space. Each of these elements represents a dimension of communication, and the various dimensions can reinforce each other to produce something more powerful than that of words alone. For example, if I declare my love for you in a passionate tone of voice while looking you in the eye, moving close, taking your hand with one of mine, and placing my other hand over my heart, the dimensions add up to a strong statement of love.

On the other hand, the dimensions of oral language can conflict with each other. My statement of passion may be made with a tone of voice that suggests boredom, thus canceling much of the words' effect. Or my words may suggest love, my tone of voice a lifeless recitation, my posture hopelessness, and my eyes a glimmer of hope that you will reciprocate. The most successful storytellers—as well as actors and public speakers—draw on this complex world of simultaneous expressive possibilities.

CHARACTERIZATION THROUGH CLUSTERS

Characterization (the portraying of a person's particular characteristics) can be done easily and directly in oral language. Whereas written language may require an author to use metaphor or extensive description to indicate how a person stands, moves, and talks, oral language allows a storyteller to use simple imitation.

A character can be portrayed (orally or in writing) through the words he or she speaks, including any distinctive choice of words or sentence structure. In oral language, a character also can be suggested with nonverbal expression, such as a quality of voice, a distinctive posture, or a habitual gesture.

Further, the user of oral language can create a simultaneous cluster of expressive elements that portrays a character clearly and suddenly. Perhaps the giant hulks, booms, and crudely wipes her mouth with her forearm. Or the nervous young child might speak in one-word sentences, use a high-pitched voice, and tug at his clothing distractedly. After introducing such a cluster once, the storyteller can use it later to invoke the same character quickly and easily—perhaps without saying a word.

HUMOR THROUGH CONTRASTS

A certain kind of humor depends on the juxtaposition of two contrasting ideas or feelings. Because of the multidimensionality of oral language, a storyteller can convey such contrasting ideas and feelings *simultaneously* with different elements of oral expression.

Imagine a humorous story about parachute jumping. If a character says, "Yes, I'm ready to jump," while walking backwards away from the supposed jump-door, he is expressing a willingness to perform a scary action through one dimension of oral language (words), and unwilling fear through another (movement).

Or suppose a character is on the phone with her mother, whom she does not want to visit. As she says with a pained tone, "I am *so sorry* I can't come to see you," she wipes her brow in an exaggerated gesture of relief. The strong, simultaneous expression of these two contrasting attitudes creates a humorous effect.

TRANSITIONS

To understand the possibilities for transitions in oral language, compare it to film and video—another multidimensional art form. In film, two of the basic elements are audio and video—sound and sight. Since they happen simultaneously, they can either reinforce each other or they can add complexity by clashing.

Take the case of the L-cut, a common film device used to enhance the drama of a scene change. Normally, when a scene shifts in a film, the sound and visuals both change at the same instant. An L-cut, however, changes one element first, then the other. At the end of a scene in which we watch our hero studying quietly at home, we may suddenly hear the cacophony of street sounds even as we still see her sitting at her desk. A moment later, the visual scene catches up to the audio by shifting to the street, where we see our hero jostling other pedestrians through traffic, trying to reach school on time. The L-cut creates a momentum for the scene change, using the audio to jar us out of one scene and draw us into the next.

In the same way, the user of oral language can change some dimensions before changing the others. Imagine that you tell "Jack and the Beanstalk" using a characterization cluster for the giant: when the giant speaks, you snarl up your face and use a hulking posture and deep voice.

Suppose now that you narrate Jack's ascent up the beanstalk with your normal facial expression, posture, and voice. Since you are narrating, your eyes face the audience directly, and your words are in the third person: "Jack entered the giant's house..."

At this point, you keep your words in the third person and your eye direction and facial expression as they were, but you change to the *giant's* posture and voice as you narrate his approach: "Then

Jack heard someone coming…"

Finally, when the giant actually speaks, you shift the words to first person, let your eyes look down as though seeking Jack, and you snarl as you say, "The giant said 'fee, fie, fo, fum.'"

How did you achieve this gradual transition? Even though your words were those of the narrator until the "fee, fie, fo, fum," you switched two of your elements (posture and voice) into the giant's "scene" even before the giant began to talk. Later, you also changed the other elements (words, eye direction, and facial expression) when the giant actually began speaking. By changing some of the communicative elements before the others, you created an anticipation of the next character and the next scene.

Time-Based Language

Written language is linear, in the sense that one word follows another. In reading a book, however, the reader can escape the linear sequence at will by rereading, pausing, or looking ahead.

Oral language is also linear. Each word, gesture, and movement follows the one before. But unlike written language, oral language is based *strictly* on time. The listener cannot go back or ahead, but receives information only when the speaker transmits it.

If the storyteller stops speaking, the listener must wait; if the storyteller speeds ahead, the listener must try to keep up. If the storyteller introduces too many characters, the listener will become confused about who is speaking, and has no way to review missed information. On the other hand, the listener may become entranced by the rhythms and repetitions of the storyteller's speech, and be affected in ways possible only during an in-person event.

The time-based aspects of oral language make it tricky to translate a story from written to oral form. They also give powerful tools that increase the storyteller's ability to engage, entrance, and inspire.

NONREVERSIBLE TIME

Because oral language happens in time, it shares some of the qualities of time. First and foremost, time is nonreversible. We cannot go backward in time.

Similarly, the listener cannot go backward in an oral story. This puts some restrictions on the storyteller.

In a book, the reader who forgets whether the story began in a specified year can, at worst, turn to the opening pages and reread them. A story listener, however, has no way to "rewind" except in her memory. In this age of print and other permanent records, furthermore, the listener's memory may be less developed than in the days when history and religion were passed on orally and when bards recited epics.

As a result, an oral story must work within the limits of the listener's memory. No oral story can have more characters than listeners can remember and keep straight. If a reader might have forgotten the meaning of a term or the name of a character, a writer always has the options of providing a glossary and expecting the reader to use it, of using chapter titles that keep the term or name in the reader's view, or of putting the information in an easy-to-find prologue. But the oral storyteller *must* remind the listeners whenever the term or character is mentioned. The listener has no second chance to hear what was said previously.

The need to remind the listener of previously given information has led to various devices in oral storytelling, such as the Homerian epithet (e.g., "Achilles, fleet of foot" and "wide-ruling Agamemnon"), helping us remember which character is associated with a particular name. Other devices include: prologues which, like Shakespeare's, summarize the story to come; songs which recapitulate information that the listeners have already heard; and statements of fact which are dramatic enough that they are likely to be remembered.

Sometimes, storytellers will present a story that appeared originally in written form. Depending on how the story was written, such a story—although easy enough to follow in print—may become very challenging for the listener.

Consider a single detail. Suppose the written story you are telling is about four sisters, Wendy, Mary, Carolyn, and Toni. They may get confused in your listener's mind, since a list of four can be difficult to absorb aurally. To translate such a written story into a successful oral story, you might reduce the number of sisters or find a way to make the list memorable. Perhaps you will add a rhythm or rhyme to make the list stand out: "Wendy was the oldest, Mary the boldest, Carolyn was bony, and Toni was...just Toni." Or you might create epithets for each: "Wendy, the bright and ready; the tiger-bold Mary; Carolyn, who walked like uncooked spaghetti; and Toni, who might go off like firecrackers." Or you might use nonverbal cues to make the characters memorable, such as a distinctive gesture, posture, or tone of voice to match each sister's personality.

To translate a story from written to oral form, the storyteller needs to overcome the limitations of oral language as well as to call on its rich expressiveness.

PAUSES

The pause is essential to the told story. Just as the page you are reading consists of both black ink and the white paper around it, so oral language requires sound *and* silence, movement *and* stillness.

A common mistake is to believe that a story consists only of words, and therefore that a pause is the absence of story. This implies that pauses are "dead time" during which nothing happens.

In fact, many things happen during pauses. The pause allows the storyteller time to imagine and react. Simultaneously, it allows the listener to think ahead in the story or absorb what has already happened. A pause can be used to create anticipation: "She turned the corner and saw her car (pause) driving away without her." A pause can also call attention to what has just been said; such a pause is particularly effective after a phrase that has multiple meanings.

The pause can help the transition between stories, episodes, characters, and even thoughts. The absence of a pause when one is expected is also powerful. It can create humor or a sense of urgency or confusion.

The pause can help develop the relationship between teller and listeners. During a pause, the storyteller is more *like* a listener. This is the time when both are listening, when the storyteller can notice the quality of the audience's listening, and when he or she may cease communicating the story proper and focus purely on communicating attitude, intention, and relationship.

In normal conversation, a pause can be a signal that the speaker is finished and others are invited to contribute. This is why we say "uh" to show we are pausing but not finished. In a formal storytelling performance, however, a pause does not usually indicate that an audience response is expected. Instead, it creates a powerful silence that may elicit eagerness, dread, or laughter. Since the story-teller does not "lose her turn" by pausing, the teller gains an absolute power over the pause. If the storyteller takes a long pause, so does the listener. Because oral language is strictly time-based, the listener cannot continue the story until the teller begins again.

While one or more elements of oral language pause, others can continue. Viewers of Hal Holbrook's "Mark Twain Tonight" know how much anticipation is created when he stops talking while continuing to walk and puff on his cigar. (George Burns and Groucho Marx used their cigars for similar effect.) Comedian Jack Benny would stop talking while his posture continued to communicate. He would fold one arm across his waist, put the palm of the other against his cheek, then roll his eyes.

A simultaneous pause in many elements of oral language can call attention to a single element that does not pause. If you stop speaking and gesturing, your listeners will be better able to focus on your facial expression as it changes from dismay to joy. Conversely, pausing just one element can draw attention to it. Imagine a Charlie Chaplin-like character listening to a lecture on animal behavior. He is puzzled, so he scratches his head. Just then, the lecturer says, "Of course, many of *our* behaviors are ape-like, such as head-scratching." At this moment, the character suddenly freezes the hand that was scratching his head. The sudden pause of that action calls our attention to the fact that he *was* scratching.

Once, I coached a beginning storyteller who had a clear, confident command of word and image. Yet I found myself unable to form strong images of her story; my mind seemed to skim over it without being able to enter. Listening to her tell a portion of her story a second time, I realized the problem: she wasn't pausing. Fearful that her listeners were not really interested, she propelled herself forward just at the moments when she and her audience needed a natural pause in order to imagine.

Storyteller Jay O'Callahan tells beginners, "Dare to pause!" In fact, the confident pause is an earmark of the accomplished teller. The courage to stop the flow of words is an act of trust in the power of your presence, your nonverbal communication, and your relationship to your listeners.

RHYTHM AND TEMPO

Written language has rhythm and tempo, not only of words but also of whole sentences, paragraphs, and even chapters. In great writing, in fact, rhythm and tempo can add nearly as much to the whole as they do in a great work of music. Yet the rhythm and tempo of written language is subject to interpretation by the reader.

Oral language, on the other hand, gives the storyteller complete control of the speed of (and emphasis on) each word, sentence, and scene. The rhythms of a storyteller's speech may be marked or subtle. The storyteller may use frequent repetition or parallelism, widely varying speeds, alternations of strong and weak rhythms, or an infinite variety of other devices. Consciously or not, the storyteller shapes the rhythm and speed of each unit of a story.

Words that might look uninteresting or repetitive on the page can take on compelling rhythms when spoken. Conversely, vital spoken language may not read well. Working in a time-based medium, the storyteller has the opportunity to become an artist in shaping the rhythm and tempo of oral language.

Donald Davis tells "The Southern Bells," a story about the first party line telephone coming to a small town. Imitating the phone conversations of two sisters, Davis talks quickly for a minute or two, then suddenly returns to his normal, slow pace to continue his narrative. The humorous slowing of tempo calls attention to the rapid pace we have just experienced, which conveyed the excited mood of the characters and their sense of connection with each other.

REPETITION

In oral language, words and phrases are more likely to be repeated than in written language. Repetition serves several functions, two of which have already been discussed: to reinforce information and to contribute to rhythm and tempo.

Repetition can also hold an entire story together. A repeated line, sung or spoken, can be like a colored string woven throughout a story. Jay O'Callahan's "The Herring Shed" tells of one summer in the life of a teenage girl in Nova Scotia during World War II. The tragic and comic events are strung together by the repeated rhythm of her work preparing herring to dry: "Thumb in the gill, open the mouth, we go on with the work in the herring shed…"

Bobby Norfolk repeats a humorous characterization in his version of "Wiley and the Hairy Man." When the Hairy Man appears, Bobby suddenly stops his normally high level of body movement to face the audience squarely. Then he opens his eyes wide, dons a peculiar smile, and turns ninety degrees. Finally he raises his shoulders and mimes running, saying "boogedy, boogedy, boogedy." This portrayal of a frightening but outlandishly comical Hairy Man is repeated exactly each time. Consequently, the Hairy Man becomes progressively funnier as the audience enjoys the precision, silliness, and scariness of the character and anticipates his return.

Repetition can have a function in oral language that can scarcely be duplicated in written language. Like the return of a melody in a musical composition, the return of a theme, scene, image, or phrase in a story can, in itself, add depth, meaning, and emotion. Bits of oral language, when repeated, can become like beats of a drum that stir us into a dance of images, emotions, and thoughts.

Try reading the following sentences silently:

The meaning of an oral phrase can be intensified through repetition.

The meaning of an oral phrase can be intensified through repetition.

The meaning of an oral phrase can be intensified through repetition.

Now try reading those same three statements aloud. Did you notice a tendency toward intensification caused by the oral repetition?

In oral language, repetition can even create a sense of timelessness. Though reading the same words twice may be boring or even confusing, hearing the same paragraph twice can create a sense of ritual, of eternity. Much actual ritual includes a timeless kind of repetition, whether of the words of a holiday service, of traditional wedding vows, or of an oath of office.

In many traditional folktales, entire episodes are repeated with only small changes: "Then the second brother came to the old woman at the crossroads, and…" While this episode is being repeated, the listener may have an experience similar to hearing the words of an actual ritual.

Written versions of folktales seldom include the full text of such repetitions, either summarizing or recasting them to be less repetitious: "Then it was the second brother's turn to do what the first had attempted so unsuccessfully. Like his brother before him, he met the same old woman at the crossroads…" These changes improve readability, but can obscure the oral tale's original sense of timelessness.

Since the phenomenon of ritual repetition is not evident in written language, it is especially important that a storyteller understand repetition's power to create a space in which the forward rush of time seems to stop.

THE UNCROWDED STAGE

A surprising implication of the time-based nature of oral language limits the number of characters who can actually participate in a scene at once.

In written fiction or history, it is relatively easy to portray discussions among four, five, six, or even more characters. In oral language, on the other hand, it becomes awkward to portray a scene with more than two or three characters. This characteristic of oral-language genres is so common that it became known among early twentieth-century folklorists as the "Law of Two to a Scene."

I don't understand exactly why this law should be true, but my experience as a storyteller and coach supports it. In order to describe or enact a discussion or interaction among more than two characters, the single storyteller usually needs some stratagem to overcome this limit.

For example, I had problems telling a traditional story in which a new owner of an estate is touring his land, accompanied by the estate's steward. I found no difficulty in portraying their conversation until the point at which they meet another character, a Jewish peasant, and begin talking with him.

At this point, the story turned awkward in my mouth. I tripped over phrases like "he said to the steward," or "then the peasant spoke," which are natural and easy in written language—even when they occur frequently. I also found myself struggling to maintain the emotional progression of the conversation, which had to show the balance among three different relationships.

First, I tried the usual solution, which was to break the scene down into a series of two-way conversations. Since this particular scene depended on the steward frequently interrupting the other two characters as they talked, this proved difficult. At last, I hit upon another stratagem: I told the story from the first-person point of view of the steward, who then had only the two other characters to describe.

When retelling an oral story, the storyteller will be unlikely to run afoul of this law. When creating a new story or adapting a written story, however, the storyteller may need to change the plot. Characters may need to be eliminated, or scenes with multiple characters may be divided into several subscenes which feature only two or three characters at once.

When struggling to present an unwieldy scene, the storyteller will be helped by understanding that oral language is time-based and therefore cannot easily present many characters at once. Just as written language must compensate for its inability to directly render tone of voice or gesture, oral language must compensate for its inability to let listeners review information.

2

FORMS OF IMAGERY

Let's return to the basic process of the storytelling event. The storyteller begins with images of the story. Using oral language, he or she makes it possible for listeners to create their own images of the story.

So far, we have discussed oral language, which forms the bridge between the images in the minds of the teller and the audience. But what are these images, anyway? What does the storyteller need to know about them in order to create and convey them?

The Nature of Images

Here is the most helpful definition (for storytelling) that I have been able to devise of this kind of imagery:

Imagery is the internal representation of actual or fanciful experience.

Defined this way, imagery includes many forms of remembered experience: the short-term visual image of a scene that lingers after we close our eyes as well as a visual memory we have retained for fifty years. It includes the feeling in our muscles of having picked up a baby and the sound that lingers inside us after a piece of music has stopped. It includes words we associate with a place or with a special vacation memory. All these are the internal representations of actual experience.

What is "fanciful experience?" Humans can use the images from actual experience to create representations of experiences that they have never had. Such imagery apparently begins very early in life.

Infants may begin life unable to keep track of an object once it has left their range of sensation. Nonetheless, they soon develop an internal representation of the object that causes them to seek it where they have never been, such as when a ball rolls behind a chair. Somehow, the child creates an internal representation of the ball that continues to "roll" to a place where he or she has not yet experienced the ball rolling. In short, the child imagines the ball behind the chair.

From these first imaginings, the child develops the ability to form internal representations of ever-more-novel fanciful experiences: the ball can now be imagined on the ceiling, on the moon, or reduced to the size of a pea.

Any kind of experience can become the basis for fanciful experience. Such imagery includes the music that Beethoven imagined after he lost his hearing as well as Einstein's internal versions of his famous formulas. It includes our internal "idea" of what it feels like to receive an Olympic gold medal around our neck as well as our early misunderstanding of the words of Pledge of Allegiance.

Fanciful experience includes things that we know to be real but did not experience with our own senses (our internal imaginings of the moment when our parents first met), things we have believed to be real but that are not (our internal imaginings of masses of lemmings jumping into the sea), and things that we know are not real.

The existence of fanciful experience reminds us that mental imagery is active, not passive. The listener in a storytelling event constructs internal images that may be based on memories but are new, creative, and individual.

THE WAYS EXPERIENCES ARE STORED

Stop a moment and remember *getting up this morning.* What is the first thing you recall? What happened then? If you can, tell this memory to a friend. If not, write it down.

Now ask yourself, "How did I retrieve my images of the morning from my memory?"

Most people will describe their morning first in visual terms:

- I **saw** it was a rainy day, so I pulled the covers back over my head.
- My husband **looked like** he was in a bad mood, so I got up quietly and went out into the garden.

Others will focus on sound:

- I could **hear** the rain, so I pulled the covers back over my head.

- My husband **sounded** unhappy, so I got up **quietly**...

Still others will retrieve their memories by accessing the imagery of feelings or muscular sensations:

- It **felt** dreary out, so I pulled the covers...
- My husband was **angry**, so I got up quietly...

Finally, some will have stored their memory of the morning under a word or a concept:

- This was **the morning that** it rained, so I pulled the covers...
- It was **a bad morning**. My husband was **in a bad mood**, so I got up quietly...

When I ask people to describe their first memories of the morning, they may not give obvious clues to what sensory mode is used. Often, I go on to ask someone, "Tell me more about that first memory of this morning." When they speak at greater length, I will sometimes notice that a certain kind of sensory imagery predominates. Other times, I go on to ask, "How did you remember your first memory of today?" Some will say, "I just saw it."

Others might say something like, "That sound just stuck with me." Still others will reveal their verbal or conceptual preference by saying, "Today was the morning that..."

It appears that we can have internal, mental representations of any kind of experience. This includes sensory experiences of the five commonly recognized senses (sight, hearing, touch, taste, and smell) as well as the less-known senses of balance (gravity) and kinesthesia (muscular sensation). It also includes internal representations of language (verbal imagery) and abstract thinking (conceptual imagery). Since these last two can be difficult to distinguish, I usually refer to them together as verbal/conceptual imagery.

Preferred Modes of Imagery

Most people tend to prefer a single mode of imagery. Unless there is a specific reason to do otherwise, they perceive the world principally through one mode (such as sight) and store their memories principally as images in that mode.

In my workshops about imagery and communication, I find four common preferred modes: visual, auditory, kinesthetic, and verbal/conceptual. In other words, it appears that most people favor sight, sound, muscle feelings, or words and ideas as their primary internal way to represent their experience. (These four modes are the most common in contemporary Western culture; in other cultures and other times, other sensory modes, such as the sense of smell, may predominate.)

In their excitement at discovering these differences, some commentators have gone on to categorize people as "visual," "auditory," or "kinesthetic." Such categories can be useful in helping people notice and understand our different ways of imagining. When not used

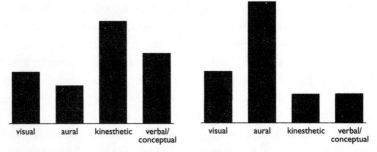

Figure 3: David's (left) and Laverne's (right) Relative Sensory Strengths

with care, however, such a typing may have the opposite effect from that intended, by partially obscuring our individuality and our great capacity to learn.

No one imagines in only one sensory mode. Each of us uses each possible mode, but in differing degrees. As an example, David's strongest mode is kinesthetic, but he also is relatively strong in each of the other most used modes, especially verbal/conceptual (figure 3).

Laverne, on the other hand, is very strong aurally, moderately strong visually, but weaker in the other modes.

David would probably be labeled "kinesthetic," but it is clear that another "kinesthetic" person could have different relative strengths in the other modes. Similarly, someone else with Laverne's aural strengths might have different strengths and weaknesses in the other modes.

What about visual imagery, in which *both* are strong? Even within a single sensory mode, there are many individual strengths. David, for example, responds most strongly to brightness—the lights and darks of a visual experience. Laverne, on the other hand, reacts most of all to visual texture, and least of all to brightness. Thus, even though they respond to visual imagery to the same extent overall, their actual strengths and experiences are quite different.

The point is that no two people have exactly the same preferences and strengths in the various modes of imagery. This is one reason that no two storytellers will tell the same story identically—and that no two audience members will hear it in the same way.

LEARNING TO TRANSFORM IMAGES

As we have seen, the tendency to label people as "visual" or "kinesthetic" obscures great individual variety. Even more important, labeling people misses how much they can change.

I believe that anyone can develop any sensory mode to any desired degree.

What? Aren't these modes just a sign of talents people are born with?

I have never relied greatly on auditory imagery. Sound is probably fourth among the four common modes in importance to me. Further, one aspect of sound, music, was always a problem. As a child, I was told I had no musical talent, so almost all organized musical activities were closed to me.

Like the vast majority of children in the United States, I got little musical instruction. Humiliated and discouraged, I might easily have dropped my interest in active music-making and become yet another passive consumer of recorded music. The difference was my father, who loved to sing simple songs with my brother and me. His joy and persistence in the face of the embarrassed disapproval of those around us infected me with a love of people singing together that I could not dismiss.

As an adult, I used books to teach myself to play folk guitar. But I still could not sing in tune or harmonize. Almost by accident, I found myself teaching simple songs to children. Thinking that I'd better get some musical training, I searched for a teacher who could teach me. Years later, I found the Kodály Center of America (then the Kodály Musical Training Institute) and enrolled in an intensive one-month summer course. Two more summer courses and an entire academic year later, I had learned to sing in tune, to sing in parts, and to read and write music by ear.

Even more, I learned about the training of sensory intelligence. My Kodály teachers believed that their task was to train the musical intelligence, which consisted in large part of developing the student's "inner hearing." Inner hearing is the inner representation of musical sound, including the ability to imagine and transform music.

The summer after I finished my academic year of Kodály training, I was on a long drive. Alone in my car, I was listening to a tape recording of a traditional banjo player. Lost in my musical thoughts, I realized with a start that I was suddenly able to imagine how the banjo player's fingers could produce the notes I was hearing. For the first time, I could analyze what I was hearing well enough to *imagine* how to play it.

Just as I began to congratulate myself on this new milestone in my musical development, I had another realization: the tape I was listening to had ended. The music I was analyzing was not coming in through my ears, but was playing inside my mind. My musical intelligence had indeed been improved!

You may need to apply extended effort and find teachers with skill and faith in you, but you can develop your ability to imagine in any form. Your knowledge of the diversity of sensory modes can help you value the ways you imagine already—and pique your interest in developing still more of your ability to imagine.

3

IMAGINING FULLY

Storytelling requires you to imagine the stories you tell. Telling stories well requires that you imagine well the important images, feelings, and actions of the stories.

You will be able to imagine stories more fully if you can imagine in a variety of sensory modes. As an example, imagine the beginning of the Grimms' version of Snow White:

> Once upon a time, in the middle of winter when the snowflakes were falling like feathers on the earth, a queen sat at a window framed in black ebony and sewed. And as she sewed and gazed out to the white landscape, she pricked her finger with the needle, and three drops of blood fell on the snow outside, and because the red showed out so well against the white she thought to herself: "Oh, what wouldn't I give to have a child as white as snow, as red as blood, and as black as ebony!"

You can greatly increase your ability to tell this scene by imagining it in various sensory modes. This chapter will assist you in imagining through sight, sound, and muscle sense.

See the Sights

What would it mean to imagine this scene visually? Since the scene mentions black, white, and red, let's start with imagining these colors.

Take a moment to call up (on your inner visual field) the black of the ebony window frame. Now, if you can, imagine the white of the snow, and the three drops of red blood on it. In your inner sight, see the contrast between the black frame and the white snow. Knowing this is a moment when the queen sees these colors so vividly that her life is changed, try to experience the stark beauty of the frame of black and field of white—enlivened by the three small but startling red shapes of the blood on the snow. Exactly what color is the blood?

Now imagine the shapes in the scene. See the window frame. How big is the window? How deep and wide is the frame? What is the contour of the ebony—curved, flat, or engraved with intricate shapes?

See the "white landscape." Is the snow a flat expanse, or are there bushes or trees under it? Can the queen see for miles across a rolling valley or only a few yards into a courtyard?

See the drops of blood. Are they perfectly round, or irregular in shape? How are the three drops arranged in the snow? Are they close together or far apart? Are they evenly spaced or are two close together with one apart? Do they make a straight line or a triangle?

Next, imagine the brightness and light in this scene. Is the room in which the queen sits brightly lit? Does the light from the outside make the room seem dark? Are there shadows in the "white land-scape"?

Is the sun out? Is its light glaring off the snow or diffused behind the clouds? Is the sun behind the queen, above her, or in front of her? How high in the sky is it? Are there highlights of bright reflection? Does the needle with which she is sowing glint in the sun? Does the queen's body cast a shadow as she looks down at the drops of blood?

Look at the scene again with visual texture in mind. Is that white landscape all one texture or does it vary? Does the ebony contrast with the snow only in terms of color, or is it also smooth and shiny compared to the soft, powdery snow?

Imagine any elements of motion in the scene. What, if anything, is moving? What are the speed and range of motion of the queen's movements while sowing? Does she gradually rise to look at the scene or does she leap up to see it? Is there a spray of blowing snow? Are trees and bushes swaying in the wind? Is the outer window swinging in the breeze or still?

Now play with your own visual perspective. From where have you been viewing the scene? If you have been looking through the queen's eyes, try looking at her from outside the window. If you have been viewing the queen from her own level, try seeing her from the other side. Now look down on her from above, or up at her from the ground.

Change the distance from which you view her. Get right next to her cheek. See her from across the room. View her from fifty feet away—then from a quarter mile. Now try to see the entire scene from the ceiling of her room—now, from an aerial view.

It will not make sense to imagine part of a story in this much visual detail. If something ever seems visually indistinct about a scene, however, you can try imagining every aspect of its color, shape, light and brightness, texture, motion, and perspective. Once you have explored the scene this fully, you will be clear about its nature, and you will have an abundance of visual information available instantly.

What If I Can't See the Colors?

Most people will have difficulty imagining at least one part—perhaps all—of what I just asked you to try. Does this mean you can't imagine visually? Worse yet, does this mean you can't tell the story? Of course not.

If you are unable to imagine some of what I suggested, you have just discovered one or more aspects of your visual intelligence that you can develop. Enjoy the process!

Try to extend what you *are* able to imagine. Make a game of trying to see things with your internal vision. If you have difficulty imagining a black window frame, for example, first try to imagine a window frame that is some other color. Once you can see any window frame, imagine it turning black. If you can imagine a brown window-frame but cannot make it turn black, imagine a drop of black ink (or a piece of licorice candy) dropping on the frame. Then imagine another drop of black and another, until the entire window frame is covered with black ink.

Can you see a black window frame now? If not, look at something black in your current environment, such as the shoes of a man sitting nearby. Imagine those shoes getting longer and flatter, until they resemble the bottom edge of a window frame. Now let vertical extensions grow from each end, forming the uprights of the frame.

Then let a top crosspiece grow from the uprights, completing the black rectangle. Finally, let this rectangle swoop into place on the queen's wall.

If none of these techniques works for you, do some sensory research. Find an actual window frame to examine. Look at it carefully, then close your eyes and try to "see" it internally. Alternatively, look at something black, then close your eyes and try to retain its image. To develop your ability to imagine color in general, glance at a cluster of objects, then close your eyes and try to see the objects' various colors. When you are able to name the colors with your eyes closed, you will have developed some of your ability to analyze internal color images.

Don't be concerned if this process takes days, weeks, or months. If your visual imagination is not highly developed, it is probably a sign that you have developed some other sensory modes instead. Stretch your abilities, but don't ignore your strengths.

In general, if you have difficulty imagining something, start with what you *can* imagine—whether present or remembered. Transform what you are able to imagine until it becomes what you wanted. In time, you will be able to imagine anything.

Hear the Sounds

Now experience the same scene from "Snow White" in the aural (auditory) mode. What are the sounds in the room where the queen sits? Are there background sounds, such as a clock ticking? Is she in a rocking chair? If so, what is the sound of her rocking?

Does the queen open the window? If so, what sound does it make? What new sounds does she hear when the window is opened?

What are the sounds as the snow falls? Is there a sound of wind? If so, is it a howling or a soft rustling? Is it still enough to hear the snow itself? Are there other sounds nearby, such as something moving in the wind or other people walking or conversing?

What is the sound of the queen's sewing? Can you hear the sudden sound of a needle piercing fabric and the sustained sound of a thread being pulled through? Does she vocalize when she pricks herself or when she sees the three drops of blood?

Choose a sound you have imagined from this scene. Try imitating it. You can imitate the sound with your voice, with your mouth, with your hands, with your body, or with an object.

As you imagine a sound or try to imitate it, be aware of its characteristics. Is the sound loud or soft? Is it sustained, rhythmic, or sudden? Does it have an identifiable pitch? If so, is the pitch high or low? Is the sound a conglomerate of several sounds, like the sound of a rocking chair (which usually has several distinct creaks as well as a sustained sound of the rockers on the floor or rug)?

DEVELOPING YOUR AURAL SENSITIVITY

Here are three activities to increase your sensitivity to sounds in general.

First, listen to the sounds surrounding you at this moment. (Closing your eyes may make it easier to listen.) Listen for sounds close to you as well as farther away. Notice which sounds (most likely loud or low ones) you can feel in your body, especially your chest and gut. If you hear a sustained background sound (like the sound of a fan blowing or refrigerator humming), listen for its parts: often a continuous sound is made of several component sounds, some of which may even change subtly but constantly. Listen for the sound of your own breathing. If it is quiet enough around you, you may hear your own heartbeat or even the background hiss of your hearing system itself.

Second, use a tape recorder to capture some of the sounds around you. This will make it possible to relisten at your convenience. To focus your attention on sound, try recording the ten most common sounds in your typical day. Or record five sounds you love to hear and five you dislike. When you play the tapes back, try to identify and reimagine what made each sound.

Third, think of a sound from your childhood. Listen to it in your memory, describe it to a friend, and imitate it. Tell the story of what that sound means to you, and of other sounds that accompanied it or replaced it.

As I write this, I think of a sound from my childhood that I closely associate with the approach of summer rainstorms: I lived next to a greenhouse that closed its windows whenever rain was coming. The greenhouse windows were operated through a crank and pulley system that sent a creaking, almost wailing sound throughout the neighborhood for five or ten minutes. Since rain was welcome in the suburban summer heat, everyone responded to the sound with eagerness. People began folding up lawn furniture (clank) and carrying things inside (doors slammed). They began to talk of the coming storm in voices tinged with eagerness, with a little fear, and with a quickened quality that suggested alertness to the moment. All these sounds were layered on top of the prolonged squeal of the closing greenhouse windows. And this sound montage was a central ingredient of a time when all was well in this exciting world—when even the adults in my neighborhood paid attention to the changes in the air.

Feel the Muscle-Tension and Movement

In the strictest sense, kinesthetic sensations are experienced in the muscles and joints; more broadly, they involve the "guts," and even our breathing. With this in mind, you can reexperience the opening scene of "Snow White," emphasizing the kinesthetic imagery.

Feel what the queen feels in her muscles as she sits by the window. How does she hold herself? Is she erect and alert? Bent and weary? Erect and stiff? Does she cross her ankles or legs? Does she sit on her feet, curled up in her chair? If she's not in a chair, does she sit on the windowsill—with legs dangling joyfully or held stiffly for fear of falling off?

What is the quality of the queen's movements as she sews? Does she jab each stroke of the needle into unyielding fabric? Or is there a lyrical flow to her stitching? Does she look at what she sews? If so, does she look at it intently or abstractedly? Does she hold her work close to her face? Or does she hold it away from her, through far-sightedness or inattentiveness—or through disgust with the task or with what she is sewing?

If the queen rocks as she sits, does she rock contentedly or nervously? Does she tap a foot? Does she stop sewing every few moments to twirl a ring or fondle a bracelet? Is she relaxed and at ease in her body and her clothing, or is she constantly tugging at her clothes, readjusting her position, or tossing her hair out of the way?

When she begins to gaze out on the white landscape, does the pace of her sewing change? Does the quality of her movements change, becoming more urgent, more aimless, or more rhythmic? Does her posture or position change? Does she hold her head at a different angle?

When she pricks her finger, does she startle? Or does she only notice after the drops of blood have fallen? Does she look down quickly, aghast, or does she slowly and serenely turn her gaze and her attention to what is below her? Does this cause a change in how she holds herself? Does it create tension in any particular muscles?

Does she feel something in her body when she sees the beauty of the three colors together? Is there a feeling in her gut, a tensing of her jaw, or a tossing of her head?

When she thinks of having a child, does that thought seem to come from a particular part of her body? Does the image seem to originate in her belly, her genitals—or even in some other part of her body, such as her eyes or throat? What about her yearning for the child? Where in her body is that located?

Notice her breathing throughout the scene. At the start, does she breathe fully and slowly, or shallowly and rapidly? Does her breathing change as she begins to gaze at the white landscape, when she pricks herself, when she notices the three colors together, or when she wishes for the child?

TUNING IN TO KINESTHETIC IMAGES

To increase your awareness of kinesthetic imagery, begin by paying attention to your own body. Find a comfortable, relaxed position, such as lying down with your legs bent and knees raised. Breathe fully. Starting with your toes, notice the sensations from each part of your body. Notice any feelings of tension, tingling, pressure, or pleasure from each part of you—as well as which parts are difficult to be aware of. Gradually work your way up your legs and torso to your arms, hands, neck, and head.

Vary this procedure on another occasion by tensing each muscle for several seconds, then relaxing it. Another time, imagine each successive part of your body gradually filling with sand. Yet another time, imagine that as you breathe, the air enters your body through each part of your body in turn.

After doing one of these exercises, you probably will be relaxed and in touch with your muscular sensations. At that point, try imagining a scene from a story. Perhaps you will notice more of your own kinesthetic reaction to it.

Try noticing, too, your muscular reactions to people and situations in your daily life. After speaking to someone you consider "a pain in the neck," notice if you do, in fact, have a pain in your own neck. If someone "leaves you breathless," notice your rate and depth of breathing. If a piece of news "knocks you over," pay attention to the muscles that steady your legs and knees.

I find myself "tuning up" kinesthetically to people I am watching or interacting with. Encountering someone who has a relaxed, open posture, I relax. Faced with someone carrying tension in his shoulders, I find my shoulders getting tense.

In an extreme example, I once found myself getting dizzy listening to a lecturer. After a time, I realized that she took few breaths, and those were quick and unpredictable. Unconsciously, I had been trying to coordinate my breathing with hers—and had, as a result, not been getting enough air. An informal survey of a few audience members suggested that other listeners who were predominantly kinesthetic had similar reactions—whereas people who responded primarily in the visual mode had no idea what our problem was.

When you find yourself reacting strongly to a person or a situation, take a moment to notice your muscular sensations. In this way, you will become more aware of the correspondence between what happens and your kinesthetic experience.

Using Sensory Details When Telling a Story

Once you have imagined the sensory details of a story, you may be wondering, "How much of what I imagined do I try to convey when I tell?" The answer will depend partly on the situation in which you are telling, and partly on your relationship to your audience. Most such decisions, however, will depend on your relationship to the story: to what you find important in it.

In other words, my imagining of a story in various sensory modes will give me vital material to draw on throughout the process of preparing and telling the story. I may never use any specifics in my telling, or I may find myself, months later, calling up a half-forgotten detail for use in a particular situation. In any event, my internal images will enrich the depth and presence of my telling.

Sometimes, however, in the process of going through a scene with attention to sensory modes, I learn something particular that I know immediately will find its way into my telling. In my Jewish mystical story of "The Soul of Hope," a character hears a universal voice speaking throughout all of creation. In imagining this scene, I had paid attention primarily to how he felt in response to a voice saying, "It is enough."

When I went through the story with a rehearsal buddy searching for sensory details, however, my companion asked me what that voice sounded like. Suddenly I realized that, for fear of misrepresenting Jewish mystical tradition, I had been shy of actually imagining the voice. Encouraged now, I began describing my own conception of the voice:

> Well, it seems like a voice without any personal qualities. It's not a male voice or a female voice. It's more of a vibration throughout the universe that your ears can't hear, but maybe your soul can resonate to, if you are attuned to it.

The phrase I had just spoken for the first time, "a vibration… your soul can resonate to" became the basis for how I have described that voice ever since.

4

KINESTHETIC IMAGERY AND CHARACTERIZATION

Because kinesthetic imagery is seldom referred to consciously, we often lack terminology for describing it. If you wish to explore this sensory mode, therefore, you will profit from expanding your "kinesthetic vocabulary." Once you have some ways to think about kinesthetic imagery, you will be able to apply these concepts to how you imagine a story, to your physical expressiveness, and especially to characterizations.

The term "kinesthetic" sometimes is used to refer to two kinds of sensations. One kind is what Jerome Kagan calls "internal tone," which includes the rarely named feedback from our heart, guts, and lungs, as well as the kind dealt with in this chapter, which is the muscular, postural, and movement sensations that can produce visible results in the storyteller's body.

The three most useful kinesthetic concepts I have found are open versus closed postures, habitual muscular tensions, and body centers.

Open versus Closed Postures

In an open posture, the front of your body is "open," exposed to the world. In the most extremely open posture, your shoulders are back, your palms face forward or even to the side, and your legs are "rotated" out. (Rotating your legs "out" is similar to turning your toes away from each other, but it happens from your hip sockets as well as from your ankles.) Your back may arch a little; your head will probably tilt up slightly as well.

Try standing with an extremely open posture. Try walking that way. As you walk, notice how your body feels. How is your breathing? How does the world look to you? How do other people look to you?

A closed posture, on the other hand, protects your guts, chest, and genitals. Your shoulders, arms, and legs rotate "in." Your back may bend forward slightly, and your head will probably tilt downward.

Try standing, then walking, with this extremely closed posture. How does your body feel now? How is your breathing? How does the world look to you now? How do other people look to you?

Different individuals (and different cultures) have different associations with these postures, of course. Some people have described the feeling of an open posture as free, naive, hopeful, idiotic, wide-eyed, or trusting. Some have described a closed posture as inhibited, safe, worried, focused, or suspicious. What words would you use?

It's possible to mix these postures. I once heard a mime describe Charlie Chaplin's famous "tramp" character as "open from the waist down and closed from the waist up." Chaplin's character needed no dramatic situation for conflict; he was in conflict just standing there!

USING OPEN/CLOSED POSTURES IN A STORY

An open or a closed posture can become the basis for a character, or even for the principal conflict in a story.

I tell a version of the "Discussion in Sign Language" folktale that I call "The Chicken Woman." For me, the essential feature of the main character, a lowly poultry dealer who saves a whole population, is that she is open to trying what no one else will try.

When I wanted to experience her kinesthetically, I naturally thought of letting her posture be open. But it didn't seem right to give her a *too* open posture because that seemed lacking in will. Instead, I tried to let her arms and shoulders show both openness and forcefulness. After some experimenting, I found I could achieve what I wanted by thrusting my elbows back at shoulder height. This forceful gesture caused my upper chest to become very open. (It also had the fortuitous effect of making me look a little like a chicken, which seemed fitting for a poultry dealer!)

I began experimenting by walking around and talking aloud in the

Chicken Woman's new body. After a time, I noticed that her posture had an effect on my voice. Without attempting to change my voice, I had found a way to give my voice some of her character—some of her essential quality. With just a little effort, I discovered that I could accentuate her "voice" along the lines suggested by her posture.

This was an unexpected boon! Now I had a character voice that I could find reliably at any point in the story. All I had to do was to assume her posture. Once in the posture, I was reminded of the "feeling" of her voice. And this feeling was not related to the incidental circumstances of her life—being an old woman, being Jewish, living in a particular part of the world—but to her essential quality in the story, her actual character: her combination of openness and forcefulness.

Now that I had my main character, I began to think about the other characters. I decided that only one had a large enough role to require characterization: her opponent, the anti-semitic adviser to the local king. I asked myself, "If she is defined by openness and forcefulness, what defines him?"

The obvious choice was "being closed." Trying it out on him kinesthetically, I found that it fit well. I tried giving him a "closed" body posture. Almost unconsciously, I focused his closed posture on his elbows—the very place where I had focused her openness. His elbows almost touched as his shoulders came forward. His kind of assertiveness seemed to come out in his forearms, which reached out in front of his body. A gruff but shallow voice seemed to grow naturally out of his stance.

Reflecting on what I had discovered kinesthetically, I was pleased. She was open; he was closed. They were both forceful, but in different ways. Her forcefulness came from her unprotected chest and her elbows behind her; his forcefulness came from his forearms that reached out to hurt others but left his elbows together to protect his gut. The entire theme of the story was embodied in the contrast between two postures, one open and one closed.

Habitual Muscular Tensions

A second kinesthetic concept relates to particular muscles that people keep in a state of tension.

In real life, such tensions have to do with our intentions in certain situations or with our characters in general. We usually recognize the thrust jaw or the clenched fist as a sign of determination, or the stiffened neck as a sign of discomfort or haughtiness. We may not recognize that a single tight muscle in our body can require other muscles to tense in compensation, or that such a constellation of tensions can convey an overall "feeling" about a person's character or intentions.

To experience the effect of a single muscular tension, try walking comfortably in your usual way. Then, without making any other change in your posture or way of walking, clench your fists. What change does this make in your walk? In how you feel? In your breathing? In how you view the world or other people? At your own pace, go gradually back and forth between tense and relaxed fists, always noticing the effect on your feelings and attitudes. Then return to your normally relaxed stance.

Now try tensing another set of muscles, the gluteus muscles of one buttock. As before, try walking with this muscular tension, noticing the effect on your walking, your breathing, your feelings, and your attitudes.

Most likely, adding this tension in just one buttock will cause you to limp. As a further experiment in understanding how muscular tensions affect your whole body, try to keep the tension in your one buttock, but also try not to limp. In other words, smooth out your walk to conceal as much as possible the asymmetrical muscular tension. What effect does this have on your walk? On your feelings and attitudes?

People have responded to this exercise with comments like these:

- I had to slow down my walk.
- I felt careful.
- I felt tense all over.
- My walk got smoother.
- Now I know why some people are called 'tight-assed.' I felt that way myself.
- I felt in control.
- I wanted to punch somebody.
- I felt strong.

How did you respond?

WHY WE DEVELOP HABITUAL TENSIONS

In my opinion, most habitual muscular tensions are *learned*—as ways to fit into our families or social groups, or as ways to control natural emotional processes.

Once, when I was a college student, I was aware of being the target of unconscious efforts to change my posture in a particular situation. The guest of a friend's family for a month, I was treated very much as a family member during my stay. I enjoyed this treatment until one day I had to make an important phone call about fifteen minutes before we all went out for a social engagement. The receptionist I spoke to explained that I would be called back in a few minutes.

When the call wasn't returned, I called again and was told to wait. Soon, I found myself in the uncomfortable position of making the whole family late for their evening outing. Waiting helplessly for the phone to ring, I noticed the increasing urgency of the other family members. Clearly, they hated to be late. Unreasonably, I thought, they demanded that I do something. I explained that I just had to wait, and sat down near the phone. Since in my family it was considered okay to relax in such a situation, I leaned back in my chair with my hands clasped loosely on my lap.

The family began a series of escalating protests—brought on, I now know, by my posture. The mother of the family stood over me, saying, "You are making us late." I apologized, then sat forward with my forearms braced on my thighs, unconsciously trying to show my willingness to answer the phone the instant it rang. The protests continued for several minutes, from the father and the oldest daughter as well. At last, I looked up at my friend to see his reaction to all this. He was standing across the room, pacing in a tight circle, back slightly stooped, hands clasped in front of him.

I tried imitating his posture. I stood up, began to wring my hands, and walked back and forth in front of the phone. Almost instantly, the protests stopped. Both the mother and the father retreated and turned away from me. Evidently, it was okay to keep people waiting in this family only if you looked worried while you did it. Suddenly, I understood why my friend often adopted his "worried" stance. His family never told him how to stand, but they criticized him until he had unconsciously adopted the expected posture.

From time to time in public places, I see families engaged in similar processes of ensuring postural conformity. Once, I sat in a restaurant watching a mother and father admonish a boy about nine years old. They said, "You are being fresh!" The child looked away, apparently in submission. The parents were not appeased. They continued, "You have a bad attitude!" The boy said, "I'm sorry for what I did," and began to suck on his upper lip. The parents, evidently still expecting a different response, raised their voices further, saying, "Do you hear me?" At last the boy slumped in his chair. Apparently satisfied, the parents said, "You'd better watch yourself, young man," and turned to other conversation.

Other times, I watch children at play teasing each other for being skinny or fat—and I notice some children trying to "suck in" or "stick out" their stomachs, in the hopes of fitting in. Adolescent girls learn from each other as well as from adults how to walk "properly" or "provocatively."

Whatever postures people choose to adopt, they are not usually aware of the postures, only of seeking (or resigning themselves to) the meaning given to that posture by the people around them. Similarly, the people advocating for or against particular postural attitudes are usually aware only that a person (who is exhibiting certain kinesthetic behavior) seems threatening, lazy, arrogant, or headed for disaster.

Not all muscular tensions are initiated by those around us, however. Some are chosen for internal reasons, to control our natural emotional processes.

When babies have been hurt, they cry. When they are frustrated, they turn red, wave their limbs, and "tantrum" their frustrations away. When they have been terrified, they shake and sweat. Older children (including adolescents) respond to embarrassment by giggling. All these are natural healing processes for emotional hurts.

Our society does not always welcome these expressions of emotional healing. Instead, partly from well-meaning confusion between the hurt and the healing ("If you don't cry, you won't be hurt"), adults often distract or threaten children who are crying, raging, trembling with fear, or laughing with embarrassment.

As a result, children learn to suppress their natural healing responses. How? One method (of several) is to tense muscles, whether to stop the process directly, or for distraction. You can't sob or shake in fear if your abdomen is held rigidly. You probably won't cry or shake if you counter your urge to do so with the distracting feeling of your tongue pressed against the roof of your mouth. In time, you can substitute a tension of just part of your tongue or throat muscles, with the same distracting effect.

What starts as a way to make it through an emotionally difficult situation may become an unconscious habit. The relaxing of the abdomen or the tongue comes to seem as dangerous as the crying or the shaking would have seemed. Even the relaxing of the other muscles that you have learned to tighten in order to compensate for the rigid abdomen or tongue becomes unimaginable. In short, you have developed a habitual muscular tension as a way of stopping the natural healing process.

TENSIONS BEGIN CREATIVELY, AND CAN BE SLOW TO RELEASE

The use of muscular tension—even habitual tensions—to accommodate to a social situation is in itself creative and adaptive. It becomes unproductive only if the tension remains after the circumstances have changed.

My first concern as a storyteller is to notice the effects of tension and release on my body as a communicative instrument. Since a single muscular tension often produces other, compensating muscular tensions, the release of any habitual tension requires a period of adjustment—often weeks, months, or even years. If you notice an unproductive tension in yourself, be gentle with yourself and patient.

Furthermore, since muscular tensions are often preventing the release of emotional tension, old feelings may be reexperienced during experiments with muscular tension. Some of these feelings may take a long time to process fully.

One storyteller, after several minutes of trying out a new posture, found it "silly," and began to laugh and laugh. Changing her posture in this way let her feel some old embarrassment, which she was able to heal on the spot through half an hour of laughter.

Another storyteller was trying a voice exercise that began with lying down and becoming conscious of her breathing. To her surprise, the moment that she began to breathe deeply, she began to sob. Evidently, she had long ago learned to prevent crying by restricting her breathing.

In such a situation, you may be facing many hours of postponed grieving. This is useful and natural, but it requires an environment of sufficient emotional safety as well as resources of time and loving attention from other people. And it is not required that you heal every unhealed emotional hurt completely before you can become an effective storyteller. Begin now and heal as you go!

MALE AND FEMALE ABDOMINAL TENSIONS

In our society, males and females are treated in certain ways that are systematically different. As a result, we tend to develop certain muscular tensions common to our sex roles. Not every male is treated in some typical way, nor would everyone respond identically to the same treatment. Overall, though, certain postural habits tend to be expected from men, and others from women.

The sex-role-related postural changes that are easiest to notice have to do with ways of holding the arms and legs, and with tension in the pelvic region. Thus, women are allowed (not required) to walk with their wrists flexed—hands held out, palms parallel to the floor. Men are not. Similarly, women may "swish," but men in our dominant culture who walk with pelvic looseness are seen as "unmanly."

More subtle, but more pervasive, are the postural changes relating to abdominal tensions. The difficulty in learning about these tensions is that one variety of the tensions (the variety you are used to) may seem "natural," difficult to notice, and hard not to do—while the other variety usually seems unnatural and difficult to experience.

Women in our society often tense their abdomens by pulling the lower abdominal muscles back toward the spine, in a way that makes their waists appear thinner. Try tensing your abdomen in this way. Walk around. How does this feel? What is its effect on how you walk? On your breathing? On how you view other people and the world?

If you are an adult female, this tension is probably familiar, whether or not you actually do it habitually. If you are an adult male, on the other hand, this tension may be difficult to achieve. For example, you may be trying to "suck in your gut" in the military style (a tension sometimes expected of males). But this is not the same as the typical female abdominal tension, which leaves your abdomen more vulnerable and restricts your breathing in a different way.

Men in our society typically tense their abdomens by tightening them from the top to the bottom and from side to side. This produces a "muscular armor" that, although it may also involve "sucking in" the gut, is essentially a stiffening of the entire abdominal exterior.

If you were standing with the "female abdominal tension" and I were to threaten to punch you, you would probably respond by further withdrawing your stomach from my fist—by "caving in." On the other hand, if you were standing with the "male abdominal tension," you would probably respond to my punch by bracing your abdomen against my fist—in other words, by trying to repel it.

Try walking with the "male abdominal tension." How does this affect your walk, your breathing, your view of the world and its inhabitants?

USING HABITUAL MUSCULAR TENSIONS IN A STORY

Once, I was developing a folktale that I wanted to tell from the point of view of the villain, a greedy man. I asked myself, "Why does he act the way he acts?" The answer for me was, "He is suspicious of everyone, and sees the world as a contest for money."

Then I asked myself, "What is his kinesthetic experience?" This time, my answer was, "He holds the world at bay with the male muscular armor—with abdominal tension."

I began to experiment with this character's stance and voice. After a few tellings, I had a character whose body and vocal quality flowed from that single, abdominal tension. Just as with the "Chicken Woman," I found I could reliably return to his voice and body.

The biggest payoff in this character's kinesthetic portrayal, however, came at the end of the story. After a few tellings, I realized that, although I was pleased he was defeated in the story, I didn't want to leave him untransformed. I wanted him to learn from the hero a new way of viewing the world.

The moment for his learning was obvious: it had to be at the story's end, just as he realizes he has been outwitted. Therefore, I added a few lines for him to speak as he underwent his internal transformation: "That's not what I would have done...Wait! The greed you spoke of...it was mine...The ignorance you spoke of...it was mine!" As I said those lines, I allowed the muscular tension in my abdomen to relax gradually. By the end of that short speech, the villain's tension—the source of his villainy—was relaxed, and he was humbled and transformed. I could offer a convincing display of a character's metamorphosis.

TRANSFORMATION IS FASCINATING TO WATCH

One concern I had while telling the story about the greedy villain is that it always took me a while to find his muscular tension. Before I could begin the story in his voice, I had to take several seconds to tense the appropriate muscles in my abdomen. Worse, whenever another character spoke, it would take a second or two for me to return to the villain's body. And his final transformation required me to speak, relax my stomach a little, speak another phrase, then relax a little more. My fear was that these delays would lose me the attention of my audience.

What I discovered, however, was quite the contrary. Audiences were fascinated by the gradual postural changes I was going through. I had learned an important lesson: kinesthetic transformation is not only straightforward to perform, it is, in a performance context, fascinating to watch.

Body Centers

Years ago, I took an acting workshop from a teacher of the Chekhov technique. He taught the concept of body centers, a slightly more metaphorical way to describe the kinesthetic realities of the human body.

Try walking once again. This time, imagine that a spot just below your sternum is your "center"—not only your center of gravity, but also the focal point for your consciousness. Every movement you make, every change in your direction, comes first from this spot below your sternum. Your "I" is located there. As you walk with this center, notice how you feel and breathe. What is the effect on your walk? What is the overall effect on your psyche?

Keep walking, but lower your center into your groin. Now, your groin is the center of your being. If you slow down or speed up, your groin does it first. How does this feel?

Move your center even further down: to a place between your feet. How does this feel? Now try an even more daring physical center: a spot directly below you but three feet under the ground. How does having this spot as your center affect your walk and your outlook?

Continue to experiment with your body center. Move it:

- into your head
- three feet over your head
- into your belly button
- at the height of your belly button, three feet ahead of you
- at the height of your belly button, three feet behind you
- to one side of your body
- to some other point you can think of.

For each center, notice the feeling, both physical and psychical, that having such a center produces. Does it have a distinct feeling of weight/lightness? Of stability/instability? Of quickness/slowness?

Some of these centers may take you longer to experience. Just take your time; these are imaginative foci that affect your body and feelings, not precise physical exercises.

Once you have the feeling of changing your body center, try changing the intensity or strength of your relationship to each center. If your center is in your chest, that center can be strong and unwavering—or it can be weak and unsteady. A very strong center that is three feet over your head might give the effect of a visionary; a weak center in the same place might give the effect of a drunk.

USING BODY CENTER IN A STORY

I tell a Jewish mystical story, "The Soul of Hope," in which Samael (the Satan) appears. In Jewish tradition, the Satan is not the opposite number to the creator that he has become in Christianity, but a member of the Heavenly Court who has the job of being "the Adversary" (a literal translation of the name "the Satan.") In the story I tell, Samael argues before the Heavenly throne, always advocating that humans be further tested, couching his arguments in terms of practical logic.

Trying to imagine this version of "the Adversary" in kinesthetic terms, I hit upon a view of him as deceptively "reasonable." In my view of this character, the Adversary may have originally been chosen against his will for this job, but in the end, he has become attached to it. Although constantly pointing up human failings is distasteful, there is a reassuring predictability to his point of view. If he were to abandon it, he would be rudderless. So he has a weary, constant, almost desperate quality to his habits of argument.

As I talked aloud to a "rehearsal buddy" (see chapter 14) about this character, I tried standing and talking as he would stand and talk. I found myself leaning slightly forward, gesticulating with one hand. As I continued speaking in the Satan's voice (saying lines from the story as well as improvised lines), I could tell from my rehearsal buddy's eyes that I was from time to time portraying the character more sharply.

Eventually, I noticed that a certain gesture seemed to help me tune in: one hand in front of my face, my index finger crooked. That single gesture became my reliable entry into the kinesthetic world of the Adversary. In short, I let my body center be the tip of my left index finger. All the tension in my face, abdomen, arm, and hand simply served to direct my energy into the end of that finger.

Thinking about the meaning of the character to me, this body center fit well. I saw Samael as overcoming his ancient weariness by directing his energy into the point he is arguing at the moment— symbolized by the "point" of my finger. His generally low-key approach to argument is given away only by the tension focused in that one finger. He appears to be relaxed and reasonable, but the energy in that finger-focus betrays his actual intensity.

In Support of the Key Concepts

Any imagery can support your concept of what is most important in a story that you tell. But kinesthetic imagery has a unique advantage in this regard because it applies so directly to characterization—and characters usually are at the center of a story!

In the beginning of this chapter, the description of "The Chicken

Woman" demonstrated how open and closed postures can be used to embody the key contrast between two characters in a story. Since muscular tensions and body centers can create multiple, distinguishable postures, these kinesthetic concepts are even better suited for embodying the relationships among three or more characters.

USING MULTIPLE BODY CENTERS

Every exploration of a story needs to proceed, at some point, from a consideration of what you love, value, or seek to communicate. Suppose you are planning to tell "The Three Little Pigs." After some practice tellings, it will be time to ask yourself, "What do I love about this story? What do I want to convey through it?" Having answered this question, ask yourself, "How do the characters in this story relate to what I most love about the story?"

Let's assume that what you love most about the story is "the practical, down-to-earth, third pig becomes the hero." Obviously, the third pig is already accounted for. But how do the other two pigs relate to what you love in the story?

Perhaps your answer will be, "They are *not* down-to-earth. They each have a different way of being off base." In this case, body centers might provide a central image for your version of this story.

First, find a body center that fits the third pig, such as in the center of your chest. Try walking, talking, and building a brick house with this body center. If it seems to fit your concept of the third pig, go on to the first two pigs. Will one of them have a body center that's in front of him (or her)? How about to the side? Experiment!

Suppose you decide that the first pig's body center is directly over his head, making him something of an unbalanced dreamer. Now you have two pigs lined up on your body's axis. For maximum simplicity and clarity, consider choosing a body center for the remaining pig that is also on your body's axis. (Choosing a body center that is not on that axis, such as in front of the body, is not bad. But it creates a complexity of relationships that you might not actually want in such a simple story. On the other hand, your concept of these characters may actually be that complex!) Where do you want the remaining pig's center to be? At foot level? Below the earth? At nose level? Perhaps you will choose to make this pig's center in the groin, giving this pig a too-earthy, sensual quality.

Now you have established a dreamer (over the head), a "beast of pleasure" (in the groin), and a practical, down-to-earth citizen (center of the chest).

What about the wolf? Does the wolf line up on that same axis, or represent a different principle altogether? Perhaps you will choose a fourth point on the same line, such as below the earth. (This wolf might be "too" down-to-earth, able to see only the practical matter of who's for dinner.) Or perhaps you will choose a wolf-body center that is not on the same axis, such as to the side. (This wolf might be "incomplete," always seeking the house-building aspect that he or she lacks.) Then again, you might decide that the wolf's great motive is a kind of abstracted hunger, and put the wolf's center directly ahead of your stomach.

You might even decide at this point to lower the third pig's center to be directly in your stomach, if this extra symmetry works with your concepts of the characters and your values for the story.

Using Multiple Muscular Tensions

Let's take another look at "The Three Little Pigs." Suppose this time that what you most value about the story has more to do with the *effectiveness* of the third pig: this pig gets things done, and no wolf is going to get in the way. Playing with this pig's body, you find yourself focused more on the strength in your arms. In time, you develop a concept of the pig that reminds you a little of Popeye: his (or her) strength emanates from the upper arms. Perhaps you decide to define this power-pig by a habitual tension in the biceps.

Now that you've started your characterizations with muscular tensions, ask yourself if other tensions would be appropriate for the other pigs. Maybe you give the straw-house pig muscular tension in his feet, making him a prancer, and the stick-house pig has tension in his neck, becoming a little stick-like and tense. Looking at all three, you are pleased because your brick-house pig has directed strength, your foot-tension pig has undirected strength that flies off in aimless prancing, and your stiff-neck pig has strength that is unusable, stifled by being directed at itself.

What about the wolf? To contrast the wolf with your three kinds of pig-tension, perhaps you hit on the idea of a low-tension wolf, full of fluidity, but a little low on defined power. This wolf is going to be smooth and breezy, but unable to knock a house down or resist a well-aimed flower-pot down the chimney.

Again, you will try out your kinesthetic concepts of these characters by "playing" with their bodies—whether alone or with rehearsal buddies. Then you'll try telling the story to appropriately friendly audiences. As you present the story or talk it through, you will iron out any problems with your imagery and your characterizations. In time, you will have a union between your goals, the story's structure, and your use of kinesthetic imagery.

Other Forms of Kinesthetic Imagery

The three concepts presented so far have been the most useful to me but by no means exhaust the possibilities. Many other kinesthetic concepts exist. One of them may prove just right for imagining a particular story.

When searching for kinesthetic imagery, start with what you want to imagine fully:

- a physical feeling of a character
- an emotion of a character
- a transformation of a character
- an image in the story, or some quality of an image
- something else you care about in the story.

Then ask yourself the key question: "Do you feel this in your body? Where?"

Most people need a few moments to consider before responding. Don't forget, kinesthetic imagination is powerful but slow.

If you have an answer to the question, go on to describe what and where you feel it. But if you do not, here are some possible ways to proceed:

1. Take some more time to talk, walk, and move with the story or character. Then ask yourself the question again.

2. Find some way to remind yourself of kinesthetic sensations that might be important to the story. Use a prop, climb a tree or ladder, push against a helper.

3. Review the story or a key scene, asking yourself the kinds of questions given under the heading "Feel the Muscle-Tension and Movement" in chapter 3.

4. Ask yourself a different question that uses different kinds of imagery. What different kinds of imagery? Be creative! Try imagery from other senses:

- colors (shapes): If this feeling were in your body, what color (shape) would it be? Would it be bright or dark? Would it be smooth or have lots of angles?

- touch: If this feeling were in your body, what would be its texture (or temperature)?

- sound: What would be its sound? What part of your body would resonate to it? Where would you hear it?

If none of this works, stop trying. Spend some time, instead, watching other people walking and moving. Something you notice in the world may fit the quality you are trying to imagine.

As I write this, trying to decide how to sum up this chapter, I look out the open window and see two people, a man and a woman, walking by on the sidewalk. They appear very different in many ways: one is tall, the other short; one is blonde, the other dark-haired; one is wearing all blue, the other a black bottom and a white top; one has a deep voice, the other a soprano. But they share a nearly identical posture: they both have their body centers in their largish bellies. They walk with their bellies leading, their necks craning forward—almost as though they are straining to see where their bellies are taking them.

Still looking out the window at them, I enjoy them. I worry a little about whether a description of them would sound unkind (I don't mean it to).

And then it hits me. They have solved my problem. You see, they are completely different from each other in nearly every kind of external imagery. But kinesthetically, they are nearly the same. So now I have my concluding thought: Knowledge of kinesthetic imagery lets the storyteller notice underlying similarities (and contrasts) that are not accessible in any other sensory mode.

Your Relationship to the Story

The story appears to be the most solid corner of the storytelling triangle. Audiences may change with every telling, and each teller may have unique strengths and challenges—but surely the story must be a dependable constant. Isn't that true?

Not exactly.

In some ways, of course, the story *is* the most unchanging aspect of the storytelling event. Once I have learned a story (since I happen to be a storyteller who tends not to make large improvised changes in my stories), I know more or less what it demands of me and of my listeners. I can enter the avenue of my story at one end and know at least which city blocks I'll be walking down—if not exactly which buildings will be attracting my attention along the way.

In other ways, the story is much less objective than it appears. It may, for example, be changed in response to the expectations and needs of audiences. Or it may be altered by even more basic factors: (1) differing concepts of what constitutes a story (chapter 5) and (2) my learning process and my connection to the story (chapters 6 through 9). The fact is, our relationships to stories change over time—even when the tales' content remains unchanged. The meanings I discover may shift and grow. A story may become my favorite, then gradually fall out of favor—only to work its way into favor again, years later, with a new set of meanings that I find in it. Even my process of learning to learn stories changes over time.

LEARNING TO LEARN STORIES

Learning a story is a process that itself resembles a story. In the beginning of this "story's story," I am going merrily about my life when one day I encounter a story. In the end, it may "get away" from me, or it may become part of me.

In between, I encounter obstacles. I find helpers. I may believe I have succeeded, only to experience failure once again. Overcoming one obstacle, I may discover another, larger one. I may be led into new worlds, or deep into the underworld of my self.

The process of learning each story is necessarily different, since each time I learn a new story, I am changed by learning it. There is a saying, "You cannot put your foot in the same river twice." As a storyteller, I am like a constantly changing river that cannot be the same when the next story enters my being.

Learning a story changes me in a way that makes it easier for me to learn the next story. In many ways it will be less difficult to learn my fiftieth story than it was to learn my first story—because I will have already learned forty-nine ways that stories can be learned.

On the other hand, a new story will often offer a challenge. The process of forging a relationship to a new story can involve me in change, growth, struggle, and frustration.

Naturally, I hope to avoid such painful processes in the future. Time and again, I find myself thinking, "Learning that last story was difficult and surprising, but surely I won't have such a hard time with the next one. Now I have learned how to learn stories easily, once and for all."

Paradoxically, this determination to avoid difficulties is actually a *source* of difficulties, because it closes me to the actual requirements of the current story.

The easiest way to learn a new story, I have found, is not to try to learn it the way I learned the last one. Instead, it is more efficient for me to approach a new story with complete openness, vulnerability, and even humility. Such an attitude allows me to respond to the unique demands of each story, while avoiding wasted effort that is intended to protect me from change and surprise.

5

WHAT IS A STORY?

Before I can form a relationship with a particular story, I must first recognize it as a story. Further, when I learn a story from someone who has a *different* idea of what a story is, I will usually change the story to "make it into a story" or to "make it better." Thus, my conception of what a story is will influence my relationship to every story I learn.

We all carry unconscious expectations about what constitutes a story. These expectations vary with the context; a satisfying story to tell to friends, for example, may not qualify as a "story" to perform in a theater—and vice versa. These expectations also vary with the audience. A well-received theatrical story based on a personal experience may not seem like a "story" to an audience expecting a traditional myth, epic, or folktale.

These unconscious expectations are, in fact, culturally based. A study of school children in the United States found that European-American children who were asked to tell a story to a large group of their classmates tended to tell stories which centered around a single climactic episode. African-American children in the same classrooms, however, tended to tell stories which strung together several independent episodes around a common theme. Both kinds of stories were often entertaining and satisfying—but the children's European-American teachers saw only the first kind of story as a real *story*.

In the United States and Europe, most people expect that the events of a story will be related in the order in which they occurred. In Java and Bali, on the other hand, even this expectation is not part of the cultural definition of "story."

The Esthetic Expectations behind the Fairy Tale

Here's another example of how our esthetic expectations of stories can differ. The literary fiction of recent centuries in European-based traditions has emphasized character development. We have come to value characters who, like real people, have depth and complexity. We value the internal experience of our literary characters, often as expressed in their complex relationships with other characters. We also expect that a story will have at least one major character who will change in some way by the story's end. To say that a story has "flat characters" is to imply that the story is not fully developed.

Traditional fairy tales, however, are based on a different set of esthetic choices. They emphasize *actions* between flat characters with almost no depiction of internal states. They prefer the vast scope that includes beggars and queens, the completely good and the utterly evil, but they make no direct attempt to describe the experience of any of them. A central character may be transformed socially (the cinder-girl becomes a princess) or physically (the maiden without hands is magically healed)—but never internally (Snow White doesn't learn not to take apples from strangers, nor does she resolve a troubling, ambivalent relationship with her helping dwarfs).

Are fairy tales "inferior" to modern literary fiction? On the one hand, liking one kind of story better than others is positive: it can be the stimulus for enjoying and even creating stories. On the other hand, the idea that one concept of story is "best" and that others are "primitive" is a limiting idea which goes against the spirit of art—treasuring diversity. Cultural creations such as genres of literature, I believe, can be understood in their own terms and then appreciated for their particular ways of illuminating what it is to be human.

Expectations About Story Attributes

As we have just seen, our idea of what constitutes a story is based on a larger cultural context. If that context changes, then the expectations of any particular story may also change.

Even within the same cultural context, the storyteller and the listeners may have different concepts of what a story should be. Some of these concepts are the mutually coexisting concepts that we apply to different genres of stories. Others are based on personal preferences, sometimes conscious and explicit, other times unspoken. They include a whole range of expectations about:

- the believability of the plot
  ...a well-developed, believable plot
  ...a well-developed, patently impossible plot (e.g., a tall tale)
  ...a skeletal plot—whether believable or implausible—that serves as a vehicle for songs, comedy, or social commentary
- certain kinds of actions in the plot, such as
  ...violent, scary actions in the plot
  ...absence of violent, scary actions in the plot
- kinds of characters
  ...familiar, realistic, common characters (e.g., "the boy next door")
  ...familiar, realistic, uncommon characters (e.g., kings and queens, or historical heroes)
  ...stylized, imaginary characters (e.g., dragons or space commanders)
- character development
  ...three-dimensional characters
  ...flat, stereotyped characters
  ...stereotyped characters who are not flat but express internal emotions and ambivalence (e.g., characters in soap operas)
- ending lines
  ...a punch line
  ...a gentle, lyrical ending
  ...a formulaic ending
- moral clarity
  ...clearly defined moral choices and actions
  ...morally ambiguous choices and actions
- commentary
  ...clearly stated moral or practical deductions
  ...the absence of explicit commentary

Every aspect of a story, in fact, can be subject to different audience expectations.

Responding to Divergent Expectations

In those situations where you and your audience have different expectations about what makes a story—or what makes a *good* story—you will need to take a broader view than you might when no such conflicting expectations occur. When I have been surprised by such situations, it has usually taken me two or more stories to realize that the hostile or uncomprehending reaction of my audience is not caused by the particular story I chose or by the way I am telling it, but by a fundamental difference in expectations.

Even so, my audience may have to speak up before I recognize the problem. More than once, children have listened politely to one of my stories, then said, "Do you know any *stories?* You know, about ghosts and things." Sometimes, such a request can simply be an indication that the speaker prefers a particular type of story. But other times, it can indicate that my audience has well-developed expectations—that I am failing to meet—about what a story is.

To succeed in the situation where my audience expects a story to be something different from what I expect, I must either change to fit their expectations or else form a bridge that will allow them to find delight in what I have to offer. Many years ago, I was hired to tell an afternoon of stories with songs to a family audience at a Jewish community center. When I arrived, I discovered that—contrary to the organizer's expectations—there were no children present. Instead, the audience consisted almost entirely of residents of a local senior-housing center who had been bused to the performance. As it happened, not only was I unprepared to tell Jewish stories to 200 adults that day, I had *never* told Jewish stories to adults—except informally. (Since that day, I have learned to negotiate with the organizer before standing up to the microphone in such a situation, but then I let myself be pushed onto the stage without any clear idea how to proceed.)

I immediately ruled out performing the Jewish preschool songs and stories I had prepared. (Later, I learned that my audience of seniors might actually have enjoyed them.) My first thought was to try to tell adult-audience stories that I knew—but those stories were not Jewish. Therefore, I tried to make a transition between what they expected (Jewish stories for adults) and what I knew (non-Jewish stories for adults). I introduced an Irish story by speaking of how the Irish, like the Jews, had found their culture under attack and had responded by preserving their folktales. Two or three minutes into this story, people began shouting out from the audience, "Don't you know any Jewish stories?" and "Sing, 'Tumbalalaika' [a Yiddish folk song]!" As the unrest grew, I saw that the gap in expectations was too great. I ended my story abruptly, saying, "But what became of Rory O'Donahue is for another day. Here's a Jewish folktale."

The audience sat back a little, giving me a chance to do better. My problem was that I didn't have a Jewish folktale ready! I remembered, though, that I had once come across a reference to a Jewish version of a Japanese folktale I knew about a poor student who is sued for consuming the *smell* of someone else's food. (The clever judge grants the suit, but insists that the fine be paid with the *sound* of the student's money.) I began to improvise a Jewish "version" of this story, substituting Jewish equivalents for the Japanese characters and foods in the story I knew.

At the end of this brief story, my still unsatisfied audience tried to instruct me in how to do better. "Don't you know any stories from the Torah [Hebrew Scripture]?" "How about a story from Israel?" Frantically, I tried to understand what was wrong with the "Jewish" story I had just told. Suddenly it dawned on me. What these people wanted was a story with an aspect of the familiar—a story that affirmed Jewish culture as they knew it. For them, affirming a familiar aspect of Jewish culture was part of the definition of a Jewish story.

I knew even fewer Torah stories than I knew Jewish folktales, as it turned out. But pursuing this new understanding of what they wanted, I could at least try to fake something they would like (as opposed to the Japanese/Jewish stopgap that they didn't like). Remembering a Hasidic story I had heard at a story-sharing group (and that I had repeated to my house-mates over dinner), I said, "I am going to tell you a story of the Baal Shem Tov [the legendary founder of the Hasidic movement]. Long ago, in a little shtetl [Jewish village] in eastern Europe..." Some listeners still looked skeptical; some relaxed at the mention of a familiar Jewish character (although a few others tensed, apparently in fear that they were being propagandized about this still controversial Jewish sect); still others relaxed at the mention of the familiar shtetl setting. I told my story poorly; the audience listened attentively. They were willing to forgive a poor telling, it appeared, but not my failure to meet their fundamental expectations about what constitutes an acceptable story.

6

LEARNING THE STORY

In some ways, learning a story is very easy—as easy as repeating a humorous family episode or recounting a favorite moment from a film or sporting event. Yet learning a story can also be difficult. Though a few seem to be mine from the moment I first hear them, most stories that I learn represent a large investment of my thought, energy, emotion, and time—from several weeks to many years.

The easy stories instruct us in the essential nature of the process, described in this chapter. The more difficult ones instruct us in the obstacles (whether emotional or conceptual) that must be overcome to allow this easy process to take place. Emotional obstacles are treated later, in chapter 16: Performance Anxiety. Some tools for dealing with the conceptual obstacles are described in the next four chapters.

Beginning a Natural Process

Think about a personal experience you have recounted informally several times. Perhaps you have told about meeting your mate, using salt instead of sugar in a pie recipe, or the time you met a celebrity.

What was your process in learning that story? Since you probably developed the story unconsciously, let's try to reconstruct a typical process. Here's an episode from real life: A few years ago, my wife and I went canoe-camping on a large lake in rural Maine. One day, paddling our heavily loaded canoe in a high wind, we became grounded on a submerged rock about fifty feet from shore. The wind and waves pushed us onto the rock more forcefully than we could paddle backwards off the rock. As the two-foot waves broke across our helpless canoe, we began taking on water. The canoe was becoming heavier by the minute, and more difficult to budge.

In the ensuing moments, Linda and I worked at cross-purposes, one paddling backward while the other tried paddling to the side, shouting at each other over the roaring wind in confusion and frustration. At last, I entered the water, stood on the rock, and lifted the canoe off it. Then we paddled ashore and emptied our water-filled canoe. Thoroughly chilled and tired, we fell asleep for the night long before dark.

Three days later, Linda and I met up with her aunt and uncle. We told them, with a tone of exasperation, about getting stuck on the rock. Returning home the next day, we told our roommate about our vacation—including, of course, about the rock. In the next two weeks, we each told several friends the story.

Months later, a dinner conversation with two friends turned to the subject of couples who have different responses to a crisis. Naturally, we told the rock story again. The following week, one of those friends was with us in a larger group of friends and requested "the story about the rock." By now, our telling was taking on the qualities of a performance.

How We Learned to Tell It

Like anyone telling a recent experience in an informal setting, we told our story easily and naturally. We recalled what seemed important about the story, then began to describe it.

To be sure, during our first telling we told some of the events out of order. When we did, we backtracked and corrected ourselves: "Actually, we tried paddling backwards before we began arguing. *Then* we began yelling at each other." In such an informal telling, such mistakes don't usually detract much from the mood of the story or the listeners' ability to follow it. In fact, they may help convey sincerity and truthfulness.

During subsequent tellings, we were clearer about the order. We even remembered more details. The process of telling the story assisted us to imagine the story more clearly and thoroughly.

How We Changed It

What happened to change the story of our misadventure from our first exasperated recital to a "piece" we could tell together with delight as a party entertainment?

Our first telling, to Linda's aunt and uncle, was very spontaneous and unselfconscious. We were telling the story primarily as a way of processing what had happened to us, and only secondarily to amuse or scandalize our listeners. Her aunt and uncle were primarily in the role of witnesses to our processing, allowing us to use them as "sounding boards."

As we told what had happened, we unconsciously reacted to the cues of our listeners. When they looked puzzled, we filled in the missing information about our position on the rock or clarified our vague statements about "doing the opposite of each other." When they began to look genuinely afraid for our safety during the episode, we added that we were only fifty feet from shore and knew we could always flag a motorboat for help. When they next made a comment minimizing our predicament, we hastened to add that we usually saw only one or two motorboats a day, often from across the lake. Unconsciously, we were trying to get them to react with what we considered to be the proper balance of concern and amusement.

At one point, Linda began to describe our argument in some detail. As she did, her aunt and uncle exchanged glances of recognition. Seeing their response, I elaborated. We had just learned something about the story: the argument was an interesting aspect of it, at least for these listeners.

When we later told the story to our roommate, we gave the argument a more central place in the story. We used more dialogue when we told about the argument: "So Linda put her foot out of the canoe, and I said, 'What are you doing?' Linda said, 'I'm trying to save the canoe!'"

As we became clearer about the "point" of this episode, we began shaping our telling of it. By the time we told it over dinner as a story about a couple reacting to a crisis, the story had a clear climax. The rhythms and volume of our telling spontaneously changed to reflect our understanding of what in the story was introduction, what was intensifying our predicament, and what all this was leading up to.

When our listeners rewarded a particular way of saying something with laughter or gasps, we tended to remember our exact words and use them again the next time. We began to develop efficient and elegant phrasing, particularly in the moments at which our phrasing seemed to have the most effect on listener response.

In short, we were developing a strong relationship to this story. We were imagining it, understanding it, and striving to tell it in a way that evoked precise reactions from our listeners. All this developed with virtually no sense of effort or self-conscious use of technique.

Along the way, we went through many of the phases of preparing any story. We made decisions about what was most important in the story. We developed a sense of the story's structure. And we began using what we learned, in order to adapt the story to the requirements of different contexts.

TELL IT INFORMALLY, MANY TIMES

To understand the easiest way to learn stories, notice some of the common techniques that we did *not* use in learning this story. We did not outline the story first. We did not write it out. We did not memorize it. We did not practice it in front of a mirror. We did not ask for formal critiques on the story.

All these techniques can be useful. Some of them can be good starting points when informal telling is not possible for some reason. But they are more difficult than the easy way to learn a story: telling it informally, many times.

Why don't all storytellers use this method? People often think that storytelling is something different from what they already do—something novel, difficult, and requiring special effort and techniques. Although special conditions can, in fact, call for special efforts, the essence of learning a story is the same easy, natural process that most of us already use unconsciously when we shape our informal reminiscences.

The Dangers of Practicing

As I've suggested, it is usually easiest to let a story develop first through repeated informal tellings. Indeed, there are some serious disadvantages to the common artificial forms of practicing stories. In our culture, "practicing" connotes doing something *alone.* Storytellers tend to lock themselves away and present their stories to the air, watch themselves in the mirror, or even use a video monitor.

Don't think that such rehearsal is always bad. For some tellers, it works well all the time. For almost every teller, it makes sense sometimes. Practicing alone allows you to be "off-line," to be free of concern for the reactions of others—in short, to respond only to the demands of your own imagination and judgment.

Yet there are potential problems with this rehearsing. First, it may result in an inflexible version of your story. A well-practiced version may not have been developed in response to listener reaction. Instead of learning from the responses of your listeners how to communicate effectively, you may have relied on your *idea* of what will communicate well. You may have become focused too soon on choosing exact words and ways of saying them. Then you may have proceeded to memorize this untried version of your story.

Second, such practicing can lead you to become less sensitive to your listeners in the long term. Your goal may become the reciting of your story in the presence of listeners, rather than communicating your story to them. You may actually be practicing disconnection from your listeners.

When I coach storytellers, I can usually recognize those who rehearse alone too much. They tend to have created a habitual "groove" for their stories. When I succeed in helping them communicate more flexibly in general, they may still have difficulty in telling their practiced stories any way except the way they have rehearsed them.

Third, by practicing alone too much you forgo the magic ingredient of a listener's attention. Someone listening supportively can make you think better and communicate better; without him or her, you lose the benefit a listener gives to your creativity. During a live telling, I often have new ideas pop into my head that I can incorporate into the story. Afterward, I often have new, spontaneous insights about the story. When someone listens to me describe or analyze my story, my thinking is usually sharpened and accelerated. Alone, to be sure, I can and do have important insights. But the story improves in unforeseeable ways when another person listens to it.

What If the Story Didn't Happen to Me?

So far, we have used the example of learning to tell an autobiographical story. The process of learning a folk, historical, or literary story is remarkably similar, with a few significant differences.

Whereas the first step in learning a personal story is to *remember* it, the first step in telling a story that didn't happen to you is to *imagine* it. Occasionally, hearing or reading a story only once is enough to implant the story in your imagination as vividly as if it happened to you. More often, you will need to experience the story in additional ways, such as by outlining it (explored in chapter 8).

Don't be afraid to use the "natural" approach for folk or literary stories, however. When relating a personal experience, you don't wait until you can tell it well; you learn to tell it better by telling it the way you can. Likewise, you can tell several people "about" a literary or other story you are learning, perhaps consulting your sources between tellings. You can "grow" your story with the same easy process used to develop personal reminiscences. In fact, as we will see in chapter 9, this same process yields an efficient way to memorize a story.

7

DISCOVERING THE MEANING

One of the crucial elements to emerge as you tell a story is what the story means to you. Although your job as a storyteller is not usually to impose your interpretation on your listeners, it remains important for you to be *clear* about that interpretation.

If you remain unfocused about the story's primary meaning, the resulting lack of clarity will make your listeners less able to attach their own diverse meanings to the story. When a story is told with clear intention, many meanings can flow out of your one meaning. Because this idea of a "main meaning" is so important to storytelling, I give it a name (and an abbreviation): the Most Important Thing (MIT).

MIT: The Most Important Thing

Your concept of the Most Important Thing in your story may be clear to you before you ever tell the story. Or it may become clear after you tell it once or twice. Or it may only emerge after years of telling the story.

Further, your MIT for the story may remain the same, or it may change over time. You may be unable to articulate it verbally, or you may be able to analyze it eloquently. Once you have articulated it for yourself, you may choose to state it baldly in the story or allow it to remain implicit. However you approach it, your MIT for the story can provide you with an invaluable guide (whether intuited or consciously stated) to the many decisions you must make about telling your story.

WHAT DOES THIS STORY MEAN TO ME?

To experience the process of discovering what a story means to you, try to tell the following simple folktale, "The Stonecutter." This exercise works best when you have a partner to tell the story to. If you have no one who can listen to you right now in person, try telling—not reading—the story over the phone. (You may wish to outline the story before you tell it.)

THE STONECUTTER

Once, a poor stonecutter worked every day, chipping away at huge stones on the mountainside. But he was dissatisfied. He saw a rich man passing by and thought, "I wish I were that rich man." A magical spirit was listening and granted his wish. The stonecutter became the rich man!

As the rich man, the stonecutter felt infinitely powerful. He gave his servants order after order. But one day the sun shone hotly on the rich man. "The sun is more powerful than I. I wish I were the sun!" The magical spirit granted his wish.

Now he was the sun. He shone down on the earth, scorching it mercilessly. But one day a cloud passed in front of him. "The cloud is more powerful than I. I wish to be that cloud!" Again, the magical spirit granted his wish.

As the cloud, he blocked the sun day after day, causing darkness and cold weather. But one day a wind came up and blew the cloud away. "I want to be the wind!" Again, the magical spirit granted his wish.

As the wind, he blew dust storms and hurricanes. Nothing could stand in his way. But one day he came to a mountain and couldn't move it. "The mountain resists me. Let me be the mountain." Once more, the magical spirit granted his wish.

As the mountain, he was immovable. Nothing could budge him. But one day he felt something chipping away at him. It was a poor stonecutter. "The stonecutter is mightiest of all! I wish I were a stonecutter." One last time, the magical spirit granted his wish.

Now that you've told the tale, have your listener ask you, "What is the most important thing for you about this story?" Other ways to phrase the question include, "What do you love about this story?" or "What draws you to this story?"

You will probably answer such questions differently after telling the story aloud rather than after just reading it. The process of telling a story helps you develop its meaning to you; the meaning, in turn, helps you develop how to tell it. Your sense of what the story means will not be a static, "once and for all" answer, but will continue to develop and change.

Please note also that no answer to these questions is "correct" or better than any other answer. You seek only what the story means *to you*. For example, in one storytelling workshop, participants came up with many varied but interesting answers, including these:

1. It's about the futility of seeking power.
2. It's always best to be yourself.
3. You can't be happy being someone else.
4. I like the sense of ritual that repeats with each character.
5. The grass is always greener on the other side of the fence.
6. It's predictable after a while; I like the repetition and suspense of waiting for who the next character is.
7. It would be easy to get children acting it out.
8. Everyone looks up to someone.
9. It helps us imagine other people's perspectives and problems.
10. It shows how we are part of an interconnected cycle of nature.

Each of these answers is equally valid. But each will lead to different ways of adapting and telling the story.

Suppose, for example, that what you love about the story (what it means to you) is "the futility of seeking power." When you tell the story, your love of this aspect will come through to the listener. You may use a demanding tone of voice each time a character says, "I wish I were that rich man," or "I wish to be that cloud!" Or you may find yourself (consciously or not) making the wording of these requests more uniform, in order to emphasize their similarity as he seeks power each time. In your telling, then, the climax will be a climax of futility: when the mountain at last becomes a stonecutter, it will be with a sense that all the stonecutter's strivings have left him where he began. In these and many other overt or subtle ways, your chosen meaning will give focus to your telling.

On the other hand, suppose the MIT (Most Important Thing) of the story for you is that "It's always best to be yourself." Now you might find yourself emphasizing each character's complaint about his current condition, saying perhaps, "I'm *still* not the most powerful! I can't stand it that the sun is more powerful than I." Or you may find yourself changing the words to reflect the characters' dissatisfaction with themselves: "Being a rich man is not that good after all…" Now, your climax will be a climax of realization or return: when the mountain at last becomes a stonecutter, it will be with the sense that being a stonecutter is really the best choice, because it is his real self. Your may even give us the feeling that, at the end, your character has learned to appreciate himself.

Incidentally, subtle differences in your understanding of the story's meaning are not to be dismissed. Consider the third MIT in the workshop list: "You can't be happy being someone else." This is very similar to "It's always best to be yourself," but it may still cause a significant change in your telling. If this third meaning is your MIT, you may put more emphasis on happiness. The stonecutter may start out—and end—with more of a feeling of contentment, while the other characters may be more and more unhappy as they grow more distant from the stonecutter's original self.

In general, it is useful for you to value the uniqueness of your interpretation of a story—rather than to say, "Oh, my idea isn't original; it's just like one of the others on the list." What appear to be minuscule shifts in emphasis may end up changing the feeling of the story in important ways, just as the substitution of one teaspoon of spice can change the overall taste of an entire stew.

THE MOST IMPORTANT THING IS BOSS

Once you establish the primary meaning of a story, you need to honor that meaning above all others. In other words, "the most important thing is the Most Important Thing." Said another way, what deserves to be given priority in your artistic decision making is the aspect of your story that means the most to you. If your MIT is not given pride of place, then your story will not communicate what you most want it to communicate.

Thus, no decision you make about telling or adapting your story should interfere with the effective expression of your MIT. The Most Important Thing may influence your decisions about such diverse elements of your story as participation, characterization, props, and even whether you stand or sit while telling.

Your MIT may change. It may even change often. But effective presentation demands that you not muddy your telling with lack of clarity about meaning—or by adding elements that obscure the meaning you most care about.

THE NEXT MOST IMPORTANT THINGS

You can have other goals in addition to the MIT. You can have even a dozen or more goals within one story. But achieving the second, third, and fourth goals must not interfere with achieving the goal that you choose as most important.

To understand this, consider a decision you might make about the story of the stonecutter: whether to adapt it to a more contemporary setting. Let us suppose that the MIT for you is "It's always best to be yourself." Further, suppose your second goal is to make it clear to your audience that this story is relevant to their contemporary lives.

In your attempts to meet your second goal of contemporary relevance, suppose you consider replacing the stonecutter with a mail clerk who wants to be a mid-level executive. At this point, you might ask yourself whether this change affects your first goal, which is to emphasize "It's always best to be yourself." If you decide that this change does not harm your first goal—or even helps it—you can freely recast the story into the world of the mail clerk.

Suppose, however, that your first goal was "It shows how we are part of an interconnected cycle of nature." Now, when you look at your idea of replacing the stonecutter with a mail clerk, you might decide that your new setting diminishes your emphasis on your first goal, by removing the story from the arena of natural events. In this case, to make the proposed change in the story on the basis of the second goal would be to detract from the goal that is more important to you. To avoid acting at cross-purposes with yourself, therefore, you need to find another way to achieve your second goal—or else change your ranking of goals.

To State or Not to State

Being clear about meaning is not the same as being didactic. It is not necessary that I state my chosen meaning—only that I be clear about why I tell the story. It is not even necessary that I have a conscious understanding of my story's meaning, only that I have an unimpeded connection to it.

CONSCIOUS OR UNCONSCIOUS CONNECTIONS

If I have not established my connection to a story, my telling will lack some component of its potential power. But I can connect to a story (and thus tell it with maximum power) without being aware of the exact nature of my connection. I can love one meaning of the story without being strictly conscious of that meaning.

For example, I fell in love with the Appalachian folk tale, "Jack and the Bull" (a variant of "One-Eye, Two-Eyes, and Three-Eyes" in the Grimm collection) the first time I heard it told on tape by Maud Long. In the story, Jack is forced to leave his parents' farm, taking only his pet bull. After Jack finds another farm to live and work on, he is denied food by the farm's owner. At the point of starvation, Jack is saved by his bull, who offers him milk and bread from its horns—but the owner discovers Jack's source of food and threatens to kill the bull. On the bull's advice, Jack leaves the farm with his bull, only to engage in a series of fights that result in the bull's death. Jack obeys the bull's previous instructions by cutting a piece of the bull's hide and using it as a magic defender of his rights whenever he is threatened unjustly.

I knew I loved Jack's relationship with the bull as helper, and that I was moved by Jack's having to cut the bull's dead body in order to obtain the magic hide. I had a focused sense of the story's meaning, but I was not able to articulate the meaning consciously. This was enough, however, for me to tell the story powerfully.

Years later, I began to understand how I identified the bull with my father, who was my great helper. Then I realized how painful it had been for me to "go beyond" my father and use his life-saving gifts to me in the service of my own goals. Thus, the primary meaning of the story for me was the struggle to accept help and then go beyond the limitations of one's helpers. When I gained conscious awareness of that meaning, I could confirm my artistic judgments about the story and solve some problems I had with it. But even before that, my unconscious knowledge of the story's meaning had been enough for telling the story with emotional power and depth.

A CONTINUUM OF WAYS TO STATE MEANING

Our understanding of a story's meaning can be conscious or unconscious. Yet once we become conscious of our Most Important Thing, we still have many choices about how much of it to state within the story.

Usually, the context of a story provides expectations about whether the meaning should be stated. In many religious settings it is expected that the storyteller (or another commentator) will make an explicit statement of the story's meaning or connection to a theme under discussion.

Among many observant Eastern European Jews, to give another example, only people with low prestige tell stories "for their own sake" or for the sake of entertainment. Everyone may tell stories as part of various social activities, but the educated and privileged only tell stories that relate to religious precepts or to topics under discussion. Indeed, such a storyteller may be offended to be praised for the performance rather than for the application of the story to a moral point being discussed.

In entertainment contexts, on the other hand, a separate statement of the meaning of a story is rare. It would be unusual—and likely unpopular—for a storytelling comedian or theatrical storyteller to state what the story means to the performer.

Yet within the requirements of particular contexts, you still have a spectrum of techniques for expressing meaning. If you choose to make an explicit statement of a story's meaning to you, you can do so within the story, or else before or after it. You make the before and after statements as the storyteller. Within the story, you can make the statement either as the narrator or as a character.

A brief statement before the story is usually unintrusive: "The story I am about to tell you is important to me because it is about the value of telling our own stories." The disadvantage of such a statement, however, is that it may prevent audience members from opening themselves to the story. If listeners think that personal storytelling is not only unimportant but is self-indulgent twaddle, they may resist your story after such an introduction.

Another alternative is to make a similar statement of meaning after the story. This avoids shutting down your audience before the story begins, but it has risks. People may feel that you tricked them into entering an open, trusting, story-listening state, only to sneak in a moral.

An explicit statement of meaning can also be included within the story itself. This, too, can be accomplished in several ways, depending on which persona is speaking. The narrator can be the persona who states the meaning, saying perhaps, "And that is why it is important to tell your own story." Alternatively, a character can make the statement: "And that's how I learned that it is important for me to tell my own story." In an indirect version of this technique, a character can make a statement from an opposite viewpoint: "I intend to destroy the human species! And I can do it, if I can just keep them from telling their own stories and thus remembering who they really are!" Or the hero's older brother in a fairy tale can say to the hero, "Why are you bothering to tell your story to that old man? That's a waste of time!"

Finally, you can incorporate the meaning into the actions of the story. If the hero tells his story and is then rewarded or succeeds in some way, the importance of storytelling is implicit in the story. This way of communicating allows listeners to reach independent conclusions—probably more meaningful to them than what they merely hear from you. On the other hand, you run a greater risk that people will not come to the same conclusion that you did.

In the end, of course, you must choose for yourself how explicit or implicit you wish to make your understanding of a story's meaning. You must take into account your own requirements, which include your purpose in telling the story, your understanding of the story, and your own tastes and preferences. Then, as always, you must create a balance between your requirements and the various demands of your situation, your listeners, and your story.

8

DISCOVERING THE STRUCTURE

As you begin to tell a story, you will start to discover its meaning to you. Your tellings and your understanding of meaning will both contribute to a sense—conscious or not—of the story's structure. At the same time, your growing knowledge of the story's structure can also help your telling and your understanding of the story's meaning.

Outlining

When repeatedly telling an informal personal story, you develop an unconscious conception of its structure: where the climax (or climaxes) occurs and how each element relates to the others. When struggling with a long or difficult story—or even when learning a short tale—it may make sense to analyze the story more concretely. The simplest way to represent a story's structure is to outline it.

An outline's basic purpose is to show the scenes of a story and their relationship to each other. Any form of "outline" that represents your concept of the story's structure will do.

One simple form is just a list of scenes. "The Stonecutter" (see page 88) might come out like this:

- Stonecutter wishes he were rich man. Spirit grants wish.
- As rich man, feels less powerful than sun; wishes to be sun. Granted.
- As sun, scorches earth until blocked by cloud; wishes to be cloud. Granted.
- As cloud, causes darkness until blown by wind. Wishes to be wind. Granted.
- As wind, blows storms. Blocked by mountain. Wishes to be mountain. Granted.

- As mountain, immovable. But feels stonecutter chipping at him. Wishes to be stonecutter. One last time, wish granted.

This kind of outline makes it clear that the story has six basic scenes, and that a pattern is repeated in each: what he does (scorches earth), what thwarts him (blocked by cloud), what he wishes to be (cloud), and how his wish is granted. A briefer form of this outline might be just as useful:

- Stonecutter wishes he were rich man. Spirit grants wish.
- Feels less powerful than sun.
- Scorches earth until blocked by cloud. Causes darkness until blown by wind. Blows storms. Blocked by mountain.
- Immovable. But feels stonecutter chipping at him.
- Wishes to be stonecutter. One last time, granted.

One function of an outline is as a reference while you tell the story for the first few times. An outline is much easier to glance at than the complete text, and also directs your attention to *scenes* rather than to the actual words of the story.

As a "crib sheet" for a practice telling, a still briefer outline might be the best of all, since it allows you to remind yourself of the essential sequence at a glance:

Stonecutter
Rich man
Sun
Cloud
Wind
Mountain
Stonecutter

A still more graphic outline puts the essential sequence into a diagram (figure 4).

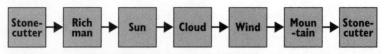

Figure 4: The Stonecutter—Episodes in a Line

Notice again that there is no "correct" way to outline—only a way that makes sense to you and that reflects your interpretation of the story. In fact, each outline can be thought of as representing a theory about the structure, based on your unique understanding of the story's meanings—especially your Most Important Thing.

The diagram just given represents a theory that emphasizes the linear nature of the story. In this theory, we tend to think of the story as a "train track" that leads from one state to another. As a result, this diagram would make sense if you see the story as being primarily about the stonecutter's learning of something particular or his transformation from one state to another (such as from dissatisfaction to contentment).

On the other hand, your understanding of the story may emphasize the stonecutter returning to his original state rather than progressing. In this case, a circular diagram may better express your "theory" of the story (figure 5).

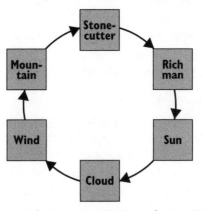

Figure 5: The Stonecutter—Episodes in a Circle

But what if you see the story as a lesson in the futility of seeking power, in which the stonecutter is essentially unchanged at the end, but has learned that the search for power just leads him on a futile digression? In this case, your outline may show the whole progression away from his true identity as a single, multiscene episode (figure 6).

You might be thinking that none of this matters if your Most Important Thing is a less lofty one, such as "It's predictable after a while; I like the repetition and suspense of waiting for who the next

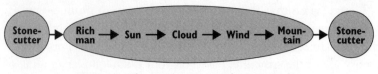

Figure 6: The Stonecutter—Three Episodes

character is." On the contrary, this understanding of the story can also lead you to an appropriate form of outline, perhaps emphasizing the repetition within each scene in this way:

1. Stonecutter cuts stone.
   Happy! Until...
   Sees rich man.
   Wishes to be rich man.
   Magical spirit hears.
   Wish granted.
2. Rich man (feels powerful).
3. Sun (scorches earth).
4. Cloud (blocks sun).
5. Wind (makes storms).
6. Mountain (is immovable).
7. Stonecutter (cuts stone. Happy!)

This outline represents the story as having two essential elements: the "rigmarole" repeated in each scene, and a list of characters (and what they do when happy) to "plug in" to the rigmarole.

Thus, every outline is dependent on your individual understanding of the story. Your MIT helps you create an appropriate outline, and, at the same time, the process of outlining helps you clarify your interpretation of the meaning.

Time-Lines

Another concrete representation of your story's structure is the time-line. In a simple story, a time-line can consist of nothing more than a horizontal line marked with scenes, as in figure 7 (essentially

Figure 7: The Stonecutter—a Time-Line

similar to figure 4: The Stonecutter-Episodes in a Line).

A time-line diagram, however, can also show certain aspects of the story's structure that an outline may not show, such as the overall rise and fall of a story's action, or the simultaneous progressions of several independent themes.

Suppose, for example, that you see the central meaning of "The Stonecutter" as "The grass is always greener on the other side of the fence." Further, suppose you see the stonecutter as initially calm, then increasingly motivated by the successive "greener pastures" glimpsed as the rich man, the sun, etc. The frenzy of desire for "something better" builds and builds until the very moment that the mountain is transformed back to the stonecutter—at which point the stonecutter, in a moment of understanding, becomes even more calm and satisfied than he was at the start. This rise and fall of frenzy might be graphically represented in a timeline (figure 8).

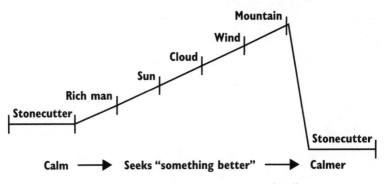

Figure 8: The Stonecutter—Rise and Fall

The great power of time-lines really comes with more complex stories in which several simultaneous developments must be coordinated. Nowhere is this power more helpful than in developing autobiographical or historical pieces—stories requiring the selection of incidents that efficiently develop themes important to you.

Other Tools for Understanding Structure

There can never be a complete book of all the ways to learn stories, because each story must be learned by each storyteller in a unique way. Each example of an outline or a time-line in this chapter is a strategy I created in response to the unique demands of learning a particular story. I don't think you'll succeed if you try to apply these methods mechanically; the results will be mechanical. Instead, think of them as examples to inspire your own methods for coming to terms with each story's structure.

Over the years, I have found outlines and time-lines to be my most useful tools. But often enough I create a new tool for the project at hand:

- I have "conducted" stories as though they were symphonies, imagining them silently while waving my hands to suggest quietude here, then a long build to a climax there.

- I have drawn individual scenes on separate pieces of paper, then arranged and rearranged the papers to "break open" my sense of the order in which the story must be told.

- I have imagined stories as ropes with strands of many colors, each coming to the surface for a while, then burrowing back to the center until later it climbs into visibility again.

- I have audiotaped my telling of a story to a rehearsal partner, then transcribed the tape word for word. Sometimes I have added a column next to the text for a list of the themes that appear in each paragraph. Once I used the extra column for a list of emotionally related images from other parts of the story.

- I have found sensations in my body, and have tried to understand the whole story as a progression from one sensation, posture, or type of movement to another. I have danced my stories, sung my stories, and shaped them out of clay.

I encourage you to use your repertory of story-learning skills and experiences as tools at your command. Use your creativity to respond to the unique demands of learning each story. This moment in your story-learning career will never come again. Be open to it, savor it, and let it lead you where you have never been.

9

MEMORIZING

A thorough understanding of a story's structure is the most solid foundation for any attempts at memorizing. Many beginning storytellers assume that "the way" to tell a story is to memorize it word for word. By now, however, I hope that you see there is a much easier way to learn stories that also leads to more effective storytelling. In most cases, you will have no need to memorize at all.

Sometimes you may have your own valid reasons to memorize parts or all of a story—among them:

- This section of the story only seems to work when I include certain phrases in a certain order. If I don't memorize them, I get them wrong half the time.

- I don't need to memorize the whole story, but the humor in this particular section depends on stating these two sentences very precisely.

- The story's author has created a careful balance between two attitudes. Any other wording (that I can think of) destroys this delicate balance.

- I am presenting a narrative poem and wish to preserve its poetry.

- I am telling a sacred text and am expected to preserve every word.

In some traditional settings, people may indeed expect a particular kind of story to be memorized. For members of the culture, this is certainly a valid reason to memorize. Still, even when traditional tellers claim to tell a story "exactly the same," tape-recording folklorists have rarely found two performances that are word-for-word duplicates. In oral cultures, "exactly the same" does not appear to imply the level of exactitude that it might in literate cultures.

One common justification for memorizing a literary story is, "I love the author's words so much that I don't want to deprive my listeners of their beauty." Often this thinking is based on lack of self-confidence or on a misunderstanding about the nature of oral language. Before you decide to memorize a story, you need to grasp that your love of the story is your single most important communicative tool. It is almost always effective to tell a heartfelt and fully imagined story in your own words. It is rarely effective to tell a story while your attention is focused on "I hope I get all the details right."

The highest goal, of course, is to tell a heartfelt and fully imagined story in the most effective possible words. The shortest road to achieving this goal does not usually *begin* with memorizing your story.

Why Not to Begin by Memorizing

Memorizing a story can make sense, but rarely as a first step. For one thing, it is ineffective. Memorizing the words of a story you don't already know well can lead you to visualize the paper on which the words are written, rather than to imagine the story's events. As a result, your special, unconscious oral language skills will be compromised.

Further, you tend to imagine the story as a linear stream of words, rather than as a complex set of interrelated images. This will rob your internal imagery—and thus your telling—of richness. In the extreme case, you will become so dependent on the sequence of words that if you forget a word or phrase you will be unable to continue without starting over.

At the very least, avoid memorizing the end of the story last. When I memorize song texts (which, unlike stories, usually require word-for-word knowledge), I first talk through the song, telling it as a story: "Well, the song starts with comparing our lives to the leaves on trees..." Then I analyze the structure, just as I would a story's structure, looking for the *relationships* that dictate the order of the verses, sentences, phrases, and words. Only then do I begin to learn the actual words—starting from the end, not from the beginning. Thus, I learn the last verse first, then the next-to-last, etc. What I memorize first will be the best learned! I want my singing to lead me into what I am more and more sure of, not into the part of the song I know least.

The second reason not to start off memorizing is that the words, although important, are never the crucial part of the story. The most important part of the story is, by definition, my MIT. To memorize a story before knowing the Most Important Thing is a waste of effort, since I can't even make a good decision about whether to memorize until I am clear about what matters to me in the story!

Using My MIT to Create a Structure

My first step in memorizing a story is to decide my MIT. As we have seen earlier, this Most Important Thing could be:

- what I love most about the story
- what draws me to the story
- what the story is about for me
- what the story means to me
- what I most want to communicate through the story

Next, I want to know the key events that must happen in my story in order to communicate my MIT. To make this process clear, consider the familiar example of "Jack and the Beanstalk."

Let us say that "Jack and the Beanstalk" is, for me, about Jack's openness to the new and unknown. (Different storytellers will have different MITs for this story; their process of memorization will be similar in form, but different in detail.)

Once I have chosen an MIT, I have to ask myself, "What in the story relates to this MIT?" In the case of "Jack and the Beanstalk," I ask, "What parts of this story relate to the idea of Jack's openness?" My answer might take the form of a list like this:

1. Jack isn't already tied down in a conventional life (such as marriage or owning property) and is therefore able to go exploring.
2. Jack responds to the unusual offer of beans from the old man.

3. His mother's scolding does not deter Jack from proceeding to explore the unknown.
4. Jack climbs the beanstalk rather than ignoring it, running from it, or trying to destroy it.
5. Jack explores the other world he finds.
6. Jack makes friends with the giant's wife.
7. Jack takes the giant's wife's advice rather than discounting her.
8. Jack seeks out the giant's treasures.
9. Jack does not let the threatening giant deter him from seeking what he wants.
10. Jack cuts off access to the other world—closes down his openness—when his home is threatened with invasion by the giant.
11. Jack lives ever after with the rewards of his newly tempered openness.

Now, I need to organize this list into the large sections of the story. My grouping came out in five sections:

A. 1–3 Jack's openness gains him access to another world.
B. 4–9 Jack finds and gets a treasure from the other world.
C. 4–5, 8–9 Repeat. Jack gets a second treasure.
D. 4–5, 8–9 Repeat again. Jack gets a third treasure.
E. 10–11 Jack cuts off access to the other world, ensuring his long-term safety and thriving.

Now I can see a basic three-part structure of this story, as it relates to my MIT of Jack's openness to the new and unknown: first, his openness gains him access to another world; second, in a series of three visits he explores the other world and gains its three treasures; third, he cuts off access to it, thus protecting himself and his prosperity.

At this point, my diagram of the story's structure looks like figure 9.

I now have a main "arch" of my story's movement and three subsidiary arches. One of those subsidiary arches, in turn, has three sub-sub arches under it (sections B, C, and D). Further, each subsidiary arch has from two to six important moments in it.

At this point, I think, "What are the three treasures, and what are their different relationships to my theme?" This might be a good time to consult variants of the folktale. Perhaps different versions have different treasures. Perhaps some of the treasures (or their order) will make more sense to me than others in terms of Jack's openness.

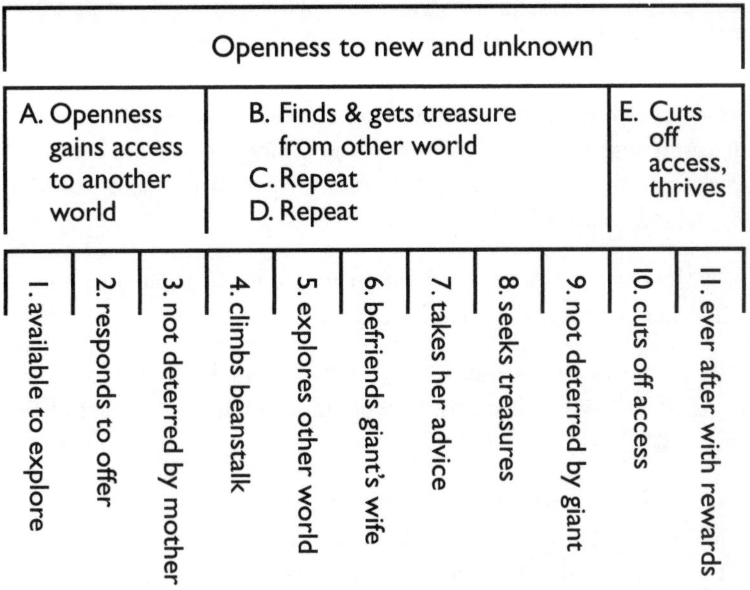

Openness to new and unknown		
A. Openness gains access to another world	B. Finds & gets treasure from other world C. Repeat D. Repeat	E. Cuts off access, thrives
1. available to explore — 2. responds to offer — 3. not deterred by mother	4. climbs beanstalk — 5. explores other world — 6. befriends giant's wife — 7. takes her advice — 8. seeks treasures — 9. not deterred by giant	10. cuts off access — 11. ever after with rewards

Figure 9: A Structure of "Jack and the Beanstalk"

On whatever level of detail I am working at the moment, I can use my developing sense of the story's structure to make choices that further my MIT—such as choosing treasures that have a relationship to Jack's openness. Each choice, conversely, strengthens my understanding of how my MIT pervades the story, and makes my learning—including my memorization—more natural and effortless.

WORKING TOWARD THE DETAILS

At this point, I can tell "Jack and the Beanstalk" quite well, after a fashion—even though I have not learned many details of the story. I know my MIT and the three main phases of it in the story (section A., sections B.–D., and section E.). In each of these main phases, I know basically what happens—even if I forget some of my twelve main moments.

When telling the story at this stage of learning it, I can make up details that I do not yet remember. For example, I can always make up what the three magic treasures are since I know what matters to me about them is that they are rewards for Jack's openness. Or, I can improvise dialogue with the giant's wife because the main point of that scene for me is that Jack befriends this giantess—as different and unknown as she is—and remains open enough to take her advice.

Now I can turn my attention to each of the smallest arches, in turn, starting with the most important. Suppose that I am attracted first to the story's beginning. I described the first moment this way, as it relates to my MIT:

1. Jack isn't already tied down in a conventional life and is therefore able to go exploring.

Working on this scene, I remember that Jack has no job. He's regarded as lazy by his mother. So perhaps I imagine this part of the story this way:

1a. Jack lived alone with his mother.
1b. Jack did nothing, and they were poor.
1c. Jack's mother berated him, but he just lay around.

As I reach this level of detail, I may become worried about forgetting the contents of so many sub-sub-sub-sections. But learning the story "from the top down" frees me from such worries. If I forget the idea in 1b., for example, "Jack did nothing, and they were poor," I can always make up something else that helps establish my first moment, "1. Jack isn't already tied down..." And if I forget that moment altogether, I can find some other way of establishing my first big point, "A. Jack's openness gains him access to another world."

Let's follow the process further. Suppose I am ready to expand the moment I call "1c. Jack's mother berated him, but he just lay around." Maybe I will fill it out in this way:

1c1. Jack's mother said, "You don't go out to plow the fields every day!"
1c2. "You don't go out into the woods and gather chestnuts!"

1c3. "You don't apprentice yourself to the blacksmith, either!"

1c4. But no matter how much she scolded him, Jack just lay in bed with a grin on his face and his eyes open.

At this point, I can show an "expanded" view of the first moment as in figure 10.

If I forget these details, I can just revert to my idea of "1c. Jack's

1. Jack is available to explore		
1a. Jack lived alone with his mother	1b. Jack did nothing, & they were poor	1c. Jack's mother berated him, but he just lay around

| 1a1. (to be filled in later on.) | 1a2. (to be filled in later on.) | 1b1. (to be filled in later on.) | 1b2. (to be filled in later on.) | 1c1. Jack's mother said, "You don't go out to plow the fields every day!" | 1c2. "You don't go out to the woods to gather chestnuts!" | 1c3. "You don't apprentice yourself to the blacksmith, either!" | 1c4. But no matter how much she scolded him, Jack just lay in bed with a grin on his face... |

Figure 10: The First Moment—Expanded View

mother berated him, but he just lay around," either filling in different details or summarizing without details. But I will always know how this scene relates to the rest of the story and to my MIT. I need only add as much detail to each scene as I need in order to convey what matters to me.

AT LAST, THE WORDS

Let's go a step further in adding detail to "Jack and the Beanstalk." Suppose I decide that the words of 1c1. through 1c3. are crucial and should always be repeated exactly as they are. (I can see no reason at this point why these particular words should be important, but later I might. Perhaps I will create an exact repetition, making Jack's mother say these very words later when she berates Jack for trading the cow for beans.) As soon as I decide that these words must be exact, I can try to learn them.

Learning the words at this point—only when I conclude that they matter—has several advantages:

- I don't have to learn all the words of the story at once.

- I can always tell the story as I am learning it; if I forget these words, I will lose their special value, but I won't lose the bigger value of the story itself. If I ever forget these words while telling, I will always know where I am in the story. I will never have to get a "running start" in the hopes of picking up the dropped thread of story. Instead of putting my attention first on words, I put it first on the relationships of the various parts of the story to my MIT.

- This procedure, which will never prevent me from memorizing exact words, guarantees that I keep the story as a whole in my mind, even as I fine-tune the details.

The Central Role of Deciding the MIT

Again, the first step in memorizing "Jack and the Beanstalk" was to determine the MIT of the story for me. If I had chosen a different MIT, different episodes would be important and "Jack and the Beanstalk" itself would have a different structure. My path to learning the story with a different MIT (and to memorizing individual words) would be completely different. In fact, the same words might be important for different reasons, and I would memorize them differently.

At this point, you may be thinking, "But I don't want to *recreate* my story. I just want to convey the intentions of the author." This is a perfectly valid artistic choice, but it does not free you from the need to make the kind of decisions discussed in this chapter. As a critic, perhaps, you might be content to stop after discussing the author's intentions and omit your own. As a performer, however, you must tell the story with *some* intention, showing what you think the author meant in each scene. Your interpretation of the author's intent has the same function as my interpretation of what the story means to me. You must still decide on an MIT—your opinion of the author's MIT—and how it carries through to each moment of the story.

Memorizing Someone Else's Words

In the example of "Jack and the Beanstalk," I took the liberty of creating exact words of my own, rather than "just learning" words that someone else created. The process is the same, however, even if I decide to tell word-for-word a whole novel written by another author. I still start from the MIT and work my way down to each moment. I tell the story frequently as I work on it, adding details to each moment as I understand their importance.

After telling a part of the story in my own words, I will compare the words I used to the words I want to memorize. If there is really no difference in meaning, then there is no reason to memorize those particular words. But if the words I want to memorize are superior in some way to the words I used, then I need to understand what makes them superior. Perhaps I'll notice that they add alliteration, or echo an image in a later part of the story.

Once I notice why some words work better than others to describe the same scene, I will understand why I want to use them. This understanding, in turn, will make it easier for me to remember them. I will also perform the words better, now that I recognize their place. With my mind on the meanings and beauty I want to convey, I can speak the words well.

Your Relationship
to Your Listeners

What is your relationship to your listeners? Chapter 10 explores the key question (which may be determined by the context in which the story is being told) of whether you are telling as *beneficiary* or as *helper.* The beneficiary—whether teller or listener—is the person for whose sake the story is being told; the helper has agreed, for the time being, to put the beneficiary's needs first.

In the following chapters, I treat the storyteller as a helper. If you are such a helper, I believe you must perform four broad tasks that will enable your audience to enter into the listening experience, and these are covered in chapter 11.

Your relationship to your listeners is reciprocal—a subject explored in chapter 12. As you tell a story, it has an effect on your audience; the more accurate you are at interpreting your listeners' responses, the better you can tailor your further responses to them.

Part of your response to your audience is your choice of what stories to tell them. Chapter 13 examines program planning, and shows how your choices may, in fact, change during a performance, based on audience responses.

Since learning and perfecting stories requires telling them to people, you need listeners of various kinds. Chapter 14 makes this point, and it argues that being creative about finding audiences may be as important to your storytelling as being creative in finding and telling stories themselves.

10

HELPER AND BENEFICIARY

The single most important expectation in a storytelling context is this: For whose sake is this event taking place? Just as the telling of a story requires the obvious roles of storyteller and audience, it may also require people to take on the roles of *helper* and *beneficiary*. The beneficiary is the one for whom the event takes place; the helper is the one making it happen. The beneficiary may be the audience, or the beneficiary may be the storyteller.

Frequently, a storytelling event takes place for the sake of the audience. This is true in a formal, paid performance. Audience members pay to hear, then expect to be treated as valued customers. They expect their needs and desires to be considered first. For them, the performers are their helpers.

Sometimes, however, the event takes place for the sake of the storyteller. This is true in a therapy group, for example, in which a group member tells a personal experience for the purpose of healing from its effects. The group leader and the other group members—the audience—are in the role of helpers. The storyteller is in the role of beneficiary.

THE BENEFICIARY'S NEEDS COME FIRST

The helper role does not prevent the helper from also benefiting from the storytelling event. Nonetheless, if a conflict develops, the needs of the beneficiary will come first.

In our first situation, the paid performer can be benefiting as much or more from the experience as the paying audience benefits. For example, the storyteller may be experiencing a sense of relief that—after a lifetime of being ignored—he is drawing people's attention. If his relief does not interfere with the needs of his listeners, he can indulge it as much as he wants. But if the audience starts to sense that they are expected to put their needs aside in order to become witnesses to his relief, he is violating the helper role.

In our second example, the leader of the therapy group may be very proud that this particular member is finally telling her story. The leader might even feel the need to smile with pride or make comments like, "At last!" If this does not interfere with the needs of the storyteller (the beneficiary in this example), all is well. But if the leader's smile or remarks start to interfere, then the helper role requires the leader to stop. He can meet his needs later or in some other way. For now, the storyteller's needs come first.

Being Clear and Agreeing

Anyone can be the beneficiary in a storytelling event, as long as the others agree to be helpers. The problem comes when people disagree—usually unconsciously—about who is in which role.

Many situations (such as the typical paid public performance by adults) include clear, unspoken expectations about who is in the helper role. In such a situation, the misunderstandings that arise are generally about which set of expectations is being invoked. (Is this performance to be treated like a stand-up comedy routine or like a formal theatrical performance?)

In other situations, such as informal conversation or "a gathering to share stories," the role of helper may not be specified and must be negotiated. In these types of situations, misunderstandings can arise from failure to negotiate or from unclear negotiations.

What happens when people have differing understandings of who is helper and who is beneficiary? Not knowing exactly why they are feeling disappointed or even angry, those who expect a different role assignment than the one being expected of them will often make statements based on their dissatisfaction with the others involved. Those who expected to be the beneficiary (but found others expecting them to be helpers) may say something like:

> Listener: *What he did was not really storytelling; he was just trotting out his dirty laundry.*

> Storyteller: *I thought it would be a good time to practice a story, but they wanted a performance.*

On the other hand, those who expected to be in the role of helper (but found themselves expected to be beneficiaries) may say something like:

> Listener: *I thought we'd get a chance to help her more with her story, but she just gave a performance.*
> Storyteller: *I just wanted to perform my new story, but they just had to critique it.*

The most important way to avoid such disagreement is to communicate clearly about the roles of helper and beneficiary. You can show your expectations explicitly or subtly.

Consider the case of an ordinary storytelling performance in which you agree to perform for a group. You expect to be the helper. In all likelihood, your listeners expect to be the beneficiaries. In most such performances, it isn't even necessary to mention your expectations. Nonetheless, you can support your conscious understanding with indirect or nonverbal cues—especially if any doubt seems to be arising. You can use a posture and tone that implies, "I'm your eager servant"—not "your horribly submissive slave," nor "the majordomo who will boss you around for the next hour," but the relaxed, confident tour guide who will help you see exactly that part of your destination that *you* want to see.

If you have any reason to believe that your listeners might not be clear about their role, you can give remarks that support your understanding of their role. A formulaic remark such as "I'm honored to have been chosen as the speaker here tonight" often serves to remind the listeners that the speaker is their servant. The master of ceremonies who introduces an act as "for your listening pleasure" is also clarifying that the audience is the intended beneficiary. Even a remark mentioning the storyteller can clarify that listeners are the beneficiaries, if it emphasizes an experience that the audience is soon to have: "I was traveling last summer, listening to stories by local storytellers. I was so delighted by one of their stories that I've decided to share it with you tonight."

FUZZY SITUATIONS

In situations where it is less clear who is the beneficiary, it is more important to clarify the roles. For example, in order to practice my stories, I sometimes gather "preview audiences" to attend a "house concert." My listeners usually come with two expectations: to help me with my new show, and to enjoy an evening of storytelling. I use my introductory remarks to try to clarify which expectation is to be given priority. On some occasions, when I expect my needs to be given priority throughout the event, I might say,

> I thank you very much for coming to help me as I prepare this show. I think I told you all that I have a public performance next month, and that I need live audiences to help me rehearse the show.

> I've made some changes to the story recently, so I may need to pause from time to time as I try to remember which version of the story I'm telling. I know that such pauses may interrupt the flow for you, but I ask you to just wait for me.

> It is an important gift to me to have your listening attention this evening. Thank you.

On other occasions, of course, I want a preview audience to react more as a public audience might. Yet a preview performance is still for my sake, to allow me to practice the story. In such a case, I might try to establish that my needs will be only occasionally evident, saying,

> This is a "dress rehearsal" for next week's show. It helps me a lot to have you here tonight, because a storytelling performance depends on listeners who imagine the story as I tell it. There is a slight chance that I'll have to stop and make a technical adjustment now and again, but I hope there will be a minimum of interruptions and that you'll be able to just enjoy the program.

Other situations can also require clarification. A commonly misunderstood situation is "story sharing," in which volunteers from among the audience can take turns telling a story. In one common arrangement, a story-sharing session is held for the benefit of the listeners, who are able to hear a variety of stories with little or no expense. Indeed, when a mood or theme develops spontaneously at such a gathering, the listeners can be treated to an unforgettable artistic experience. Alternatively, a story-sharing session might be held for the benefit of the storytellers, who gain an informal audience for their work.

Because either expectation is reasonable, and because such occasions often lack a facilitator, such events are quite likely to leave many people dissatisfied. For this reason, a facilitator who states the expectations at the start can make a huge difference. Lacking a facilitator, an individual teller can clarify things for at least a single story, perhaps saying:

> I've told this story many times. I don't want your help with it. I hope you will just enjoy it. (Or: I hope you will take it as a gift from me. Or: I dedicate it to the memory of a former member of this group...)

Before telling your story as beneficiary, on the other hand, you might say something like this:

> I'd like your help with the story I'm about to tell. It's a new story (Or: It's a story I have not told for years. Or: It's a story I have just adapted in this way...) and I need experience telling it. (Or: I would like to hear any thoughts about how to make it better after the evening is over.) Are you willing to hear a story that's not polished yet? (Or: I'd appreciate a few minutes of feed-back after my telling. Is that all right with the group?)

If a story-sharing event can include an explicit statement of who is the primary beneficiary (and consent by those expected to be the helpers), the chances increase that everyone will proceed with the same expectations, and therefore leave satisfied.

AFTER THE PERFORMANCE

Here is a common, confusing situation that can be made clear by an understanding of the roles of helper and beneficiary. Suppose you are the storyteller in a typical performance setting. You accept that you are in the role of helper. You tell your stories, receive your applause, and acknowledge your audience from the stage. You feel, "I did my job, and now I'm done!"

At this point, a few audience members come up to thank you. You are glad. At last, it seems that someone is about to help you.

Some audience members are, in fact, articulate and enthusiastic in their praise of you and your performance. Just as you lower your defenses completely, someone says, "Have you heard Garrison Keillor? You should hear him. He can *really* tell stories." Receiving an implied negative comparison when you had been expecting praise, you feel crushed and betrayed.

What went wrong? You thought you had become the beneficiary, but the audience members were still acting as though you were their helper! It is possible that the person who spoke of Garrison Keillor was intentionally putting you down, but it is more likely that she is merely using your attention to make the connection in her mind between you and the other storyteller she knows. In short, she is using your helpful attention to process her new understanding of the category "storyteller."

In fact, whenever audience members come up to speak to you, they come *as beneficiaries*. Thanking you is part of accepting your help; giving thanks completes the acceptance of the gift you have given them. It is understandable that you become confused by their apparent offer to be your helpers. But, unless you or they make an explicit statement to the contrary, you can assume that they still regard you as the helper.

If you treat them as *your* helpers—by asking for reassurance, for example—some will switch roles and rise to the occasion. But most will expect to remain as beneficiary. If you persist, they may even resent your attempts to switch roles. Without an understanding of the role-issues involved, they may interpret their uneasy feelings as being caused by your characteristics or intentions. They may leave thinking, "He's a good storyteller, but he's insecure," or "I wonder what she wants from me?"

Does this mean that you are stuck in the helper role until everyone goes home? No. You can make an explicit change in this role, saying something like, "I'd love to hear what you thought of the performance. But I need some time to myself right now. (Or: I need some time with my husband/wife/coach/support team. Or: I have to attend to another obligation.) Please excuse me."

In general, I face audience members who approach me after a performance with the understanding that they still look to me as their helper. I keep in mind that I have choices, including the choice to listen as helper. Even while in that role, I can choose not to offer any particular kind of help. And when I want to stop being the helper, I can make an explicit statement to that effect. Until then, I operate with the clarity that comes from understanding my audience's likely expectations.

STATING THE EXPECTATIONS

In many contexts, it makes sense for the storyteller to state the expectations for an event. Except when a master of ceremonies, facilitator, or "introducer" is present, the teller may be the person best situated to clarify the expectations. Further, it only makes sense to expect to be the beneficiary when someone else has agreed (tacitly or explicitly) to be the helper. The teller is usually in a good position either to ask the listeners if they are willing to help or to remind them that the teller has agreed to be the helper.

When a storyteller is telling to a captive audience, the roles of helper and beneficiary can be especially tricky. If I am telling a story for the "benefit" of people who don't want to be there—such as those in any kind of institution (like students or prisoners), or those who are there as part of fulfilling another role (like employees at a required event)—it may be difficult to agree on expectations. As a result, it often makes sense for a storyteller to communicate quickly what the intended benefit is to the audience. Then the audience will be in a position to agree to be "benefited."

School children often expect that in any event when an adult stands at the front of the room they will be "instructed" or expected to obey orders or cajoled or insulted. Since I believe I have something more pleasing to offer them, I consider it my first responsibility to clarify the purpose of this event. With older children I occasionally try to explain what I'm about to do. More often, I offer a sample—preferably a brief story that requires no more cooperation than they are at first willing to offer me.

With preschoolers and early elementary students, on the other hand, I often begin with something silly that puts me in a vulnerable role. For example, I may pretend not to know how to hold my guitar; asking for their help, I comically misunderstand their instructions to me. Since few adults in their lives take the role of someone less powerful or less informed, my silliness signals the children that I am not choosing one of the common adult roles. Since I am making them laugh without expecting anything particular of them, I am demonstrating that I am there for their benefit.

Moving from Beneficiary to Helper

Before I can tell a story as helper, I must usually tell it first as beneficiary.

Telling a new story to listeners almost always requires that they be in the role of helper. I tell my story-in-progress to my helpers, as many times as necessary. At some point, I decide I am ready to offer the story for the benefit my audience. Only then can I tell it as helper.

TELLING A NEW STORY AS BENEFICIARY

When I tell a story for the first time, I am not usually able to put my listeners' needs first. I am too absorbed with imagining, interpreting, and reacting to the story. I may be searching for words. I may not be entirely clear about what happens in the story or what it means to me. In short, I am almost always telling it for my own benefit, and my listeners must agree to help.

The audience for my new personal story may be a friend who asks, "How was your vacation?" The friend's agreement to be my helper may be implicit in that question—but the exact kind of help he or she will give depends on the friend and our relationship. A friend or coworker may listen to certain kinds of stories for certain lengths of time and will offer certain kinds of responses. A spouse or other family member will probably listen and respond in different ways.

A rehearsal buddy makes an explicit agreement to help me with stories by listening and offering appreciations and suggestions. Even so, certain rehearsal buddies will be better listeners for certain stories, since their interests, experiences, and emotional state will make them better able to pay attention to certain stories or certain ways of telling them.

Part of the process of learning a story may involve coming to terms with the emotions expressed in the story or with the feelings I have about the story. To work on the emotional component of a story, I may need to express my own emotions. This will require a helper who can listen not only when I talk but also when I cry, shake, rage, yawn, or laugh.

When I have a story that moves me deeply, I take it first to a helper who is happy to let me express feelings during the telling of the story. I may tell the whole story, then be overcome by feelings. Or I may stop in the middle to giggle. Or I may never tell the story, but just talk about what it means to me (or even just think about what it means) as my tears flow, letting the story work its healing gift while I imagine its events.

For example, I tell a Hasidic tale about the great rebbe, Zusia, who was terrified of facing the angels after his death, for he knew they would ask him a single question about his life. He knew they would not ask him why he had not been Moses or Joshua, but they would demand of him: "Why weren't you Zusia?"

This story has been a healing story for me. Although it takes less than three minutes to tell, I have often spent a full hour crying over it. In that hour, I may actually tell the story only once. I may imagine the story, repeat a single line, or speak about what the story brings up for me.

Before I ever told this story in public, I cried about it for several one-hour sessions, in the company of a helping listener. A year or two after I began performing it, I was telling it in a concert situation when I felt my tears welling up again. I was perfectly able to go on, but this was my signal that I needed to arrange some more tellings as beneficiary. Twice more, in the years that followed, I have returned to telling this story as beneficiary.

DECIDING TO TELL AS HELPER

Once I have allowed a story to heal me, I can make a decision about telling it for the sake of others. To decide whether to tell it in performance, I have to answer two questions. First, am I ready to tell it with my attention on my audience's needs rather than on my own? Second, will it be a true gift for them?

Years ago, I worked for months on a literary story about male violence against women. When I told it as beneficiary, the story helped me face my feelings of horror and powerlessness about being cast in the role of oppressor. After many private tellings, I felt able to tell the story as helper.

When I finally performed the story in public, however, I realized that it did not have the effect on others that it had on me. It seemed to remind many women of being victimized without helping them regain their power. Most men who listened to the story felt accused rather than liberated.

Clearly, this was a story that could help me grow by telling it, but that others would not gain by listening to. After a single public performance, I dropped it from my repertory.

I could make such a clear decision not to tell the story, in part, because I had learned about its healing effects first-hand. Once I have let a story work for me as beneficiary, I find it much easier to judge whether it is working for others.

Sometimes a story that I worry is only working for me turns out to benefit others. For the first twelve years of working on-and-off with "The Soul of Hope," I was periodically ready to discard it. A few people, however, told me how this story had been transformative for them. That was enough to keep me pursuing it, and eventually I discovered that I simply had not yet told the story enough as beneficiary. Once I let it help me heal more of my old hurts, I was able to offer it as a helpful gift to my audiences.

SPECIAL PROBLEMS WITH PERSONAL STORIES

When telling a personal (autobiographical or family) story, we may encounter some particular problems with regard to the roles of helper and beneficiary. In particular, it may be more difficult for us—and for our audience—to judge whether we are honestly telling as helper.

As linguist William Labov has noted, anyone telling a personal experience story—in most contemporary cultures, even in conversation—dreads the question from listeners, "So what?" We feel that we must justify the value of a story, convincing our listeners that it is worthwhile for them to hear it. Telling a traditional or historical story provides some built-in justification for demanding our audience's attention, but telling a personal story may leave us without an external source of validation.

This problem is intensified by our cultural habit of vying for each other's attention in order to process our personal experiences. In almost any conversational gathering, people hunger for the attention of the group. Someone will start to tell of an experience, hoping to use the group's attention in order to relieve the relevant emotional tensions: "I just fell on the steps on the way in. I didn't really hurt myself, but for a moment..." In many cases, someone else will be reminded of an experience that also needs telling, and will interrupt with it, saying perhaps, "Yeah. My father fell last winter and broke his hip. Ever since then, he's been afraid to go out of the house without help. Why, last month alone, I..." As a result, no one—or only the most aggressive—actually gets a turn to be listened to. This often leaves others feeling resentful, and resentful listening is not really listening.

Storytelling is one way to resolve this competition for attention, because it creates a structure in which one person gets an uninterrupted turn. Because of the general shortage of such opportunities, however, some people will misuse the chance. Others will be resentful even of an appropriate use of their attention. As a result, clarity about the roles of helper and beneficiary is especially important when telling personal stories.

We need to understand two points. First, others *can* listen as helpers, provided we obtain their permission for a given time period. Whatever attention lapses we may have experienced before, we now have an opportunity to get willing listeners!

Second, we need to be careful with our willing listeners. We may find ourselves tempted to tell "just a little more" of what we need listened to, even though others may still be awaiting their turns or a return to the other roles in their lives. Conversely, some of us may find it difficult to ask for a turn at all, fearing to appear selfish or self-aggrandizing.

When it is time to tell a personal story in the role of helper, I find it useful to ask my helpers first whether *they* think I'm ready. If so, I ask them what benefit they have received from it. If their answers jibe with my own opinions, I proceed. If not, I take some more time to tell the story as beneficiary, or else I try it out on a forgiving audience and then solicit their responses.

WHEN THE FEELINGS SURPRISE ME

A common question from storytellers is, "What do I do when I am overwhelmed by emotion in the middle of a performance?" Sometimes, the issue underlying this question is that the teller feels uncomfortable facing her emotions.

More often, however, the teller is saying, in effect, "The story becomes momentarily so moving to me that I can't continue to tell as helper." In such a case, the answer may lie in understanding that the role of helper can be temporarily renegotiated.

As the earlier parts of this chapter explain, before I try to tell a story as helper, I usually need to tell it as beneficiary. Depending on the story, I may need one silent telling as beneficiary or a hundred shared ones.

No matter how much time I have taken to tell a story as beneficiary, however, I may still have an occasional moment in performance when the feelings overwhelm me and I am unable to go on. In this moment, I can adjust my agreement with my audience—without reneging completely.

If I am unable to proceed as helper, I stop a moment. I indicate in some way that I am taking a small "time out." I may say, "I'll be ready in a minute." Or I may pick up a glass of water, or hold up a single finger as if to say "just a minute," or change my posture and step off to the side.

During this pause, I step out of the role of helper temporarily, and pay attention to my own needs. I notice the feeling, letting it flow through me. If necessary, I remind myself of my current reality: for example, that I am not helpless or in danger at the moment. Then I call to mind what I hope to offer to my listeners through telling this story. Finally, I return my attention to my audience, and step back into the helper role. Clarity about my role itself lets me deal responsibly with stories that have the greatest emotional power.

11
THE FOUR TASKS

When performing for an audience, I think of my four key jobs as:
uniting
inviting
offering
acknowledging

As the storyteller (in the role of helper), I am like a tour leader through a historic building. First, I greet my guests and get them in one place, ready to start the tour *(I unite them as an audience)*. Next, I take them from room to room. In each room, I first give them an introduction that will draw them into the room *(I invite them)*; then I let them experience the room on their own *(I offer them what I want to share)*. Finally, I gather them up again, elicit their reactions, then usher them out of the building *(I acknowledge them, then indicate that it's time to function as individuals again)*.

Uniting

Depending on the storytelling context, uniting my audience may already be done for me, or it may be my most difficult task. In order to take on the role of story-listeners, my audience members must agree to the (usually unspoken) rules. They must agree to listen to me, not to tell their own stories unless invited. Above all, they must agree to be addressed as a group, and to respond as group members rather than as individuals.

In traditional theatrical settings, the audience is united by several elements in the setting. The audience space is well-defined and must be entered intentionally; the chairs all face the performer; the lights direct everyone's attention to the performer; and the curtain-rise or light-dimming gives a signal to stop behaving as individuals and begin responding as a group. In such a setting, the task of uniting the audience is nearly accomplished before the performer enters the performance space.

In other settings, the audience may already have been united by a master of ceremonies or by a previous performer.

In many informal settings, on the other hand, the storyteller may need to go through several steps in order to unite the audience. Listeners may need to change their positions or orientation in space, stop some other activity, and perhaps negotiate before giving consent to become an audience, as in this dialogue:

"Wanna hear the latest about my boss?"

"Naw, I'm off to lunch."

"I'll come with you. We can sit by the windows where it's quiet."

"Okay. Shoot."

Most settings in which I tell stories fall somewhere in between the theatrical and the freeform informal—such as in a coffeehouse or at a faculty meeting. In these cases, the audience has usually been gathered physically, and the room is usually closed off from other people as well as from distracting sights and sounds. Someone else may even have the job of introducing me, thus signaling the beginning of the storytelling event.

WAYS TO UNITE

Is the audience united yet? Probably not. Even in a formal theater, I usually have more to do in order to unite my listeners. I need to cause them to stop acting as individuals, to willingly offer their attention to me.

How can I accomplish this? Each storyteller seems to have a preferred method. Storyteller Jay O'Callahan loves to start with a startling sound. Sound is nondirectional, so it communicates to those who are not yet looking at Jay. It is expressive but nonverbal, so it helps Jay's listeners start responding to the cues that are central to his performances. And the sounds he creates are evocative. They are intriguing enough to make listeners offer their attention, and puzzling enough to suggest "leaning back" (discussed in chapter 12).

Many storytellers, on the other hand, unite the audience by talk-ing to them. They begin with some chatty comments that suggest a conversational context—counting on the formal aspects of the set-ting to prevent too many people from chatting back. In this way, such storytellers get your attention as a listener in much the same way a stranger might get your attention from across the street by waving at you and saying, "Hello!" You would probably turn toward the speaker, stop your current conversation and pause for a moment, awaiting an explanation of why this stranger hailed you. Storytellers who begin by chatting with the audience make use of this same response.

The next time you are in the audience with such storytellers, notice how they proceed from the chatting mode to the storytelling mode. They may accept chatty comments back from the audience for a while, but soon they shift their posture, language, or tone of voice to signal a shift in your expected behavior. Once they begin an actual story, they will be less likely to respond to a comment from the audience—or, if they respond, they may incorporate their response into their narrative in a way that signals tactfully, "From now on, I will be the one to do all the talking."

Because I began my performing career as a folk singer, the most comfortable way for me to unite the audience is usually to get them singing. I might sing the first verse or two of a song to get their attention, but then I ask them to sing with me. As soon as they comply (if they do!) they have become a united audience.

Adults can be counted on to know a repertory of signals to which they'll respond by becoming an audience, although the signals and responses will vary in different cultures and contexts. Young chil-dren, on the other hand, may not know the rules. When I tell stories on several occasions to the same group of young children, part of my job is to establish a signal that will help individual boys and girls become an audience. I always start with the same signal for a partic-ular group, whether it is singing a particular song, playing a few notes on the penny whistle, or taking my place on the "storytelling chair." Other storytellers use similar devices, such as picking up the "storytelling stick," dimming the room lights, lighting a candle, or repeating a particular poem or chant.

The process of uniting an audience can take many minutes, or it can happen in a single dramatic instant. Once it is complete, however, a distinct, if ineffable, change has happened in the room.

How can I describe the sensation of standing before a united audience? It is like the moment when the bus approaches a crowded bus stop, and the undefined crowd of potential passengers suddenly begins to act as a group. Or it is like what happens when a conductor taps the music stand and the orchestra members pick up their instruments and await the downbeat. Or maybe it is like the moment that a timeout ends on a sports field, and the players stop acting as individuals and once again become a team.

Sometimes it even seems as though each member of the audience has offered up a portion of his or her invisible "energy" to form a pool that the storyteller may then shape during the performance. At the end of the performance, the listeners "reabsorb" their energy and function again as self-contained individuals.

The pool of energy can be an abstract metaphor, or it can seem palpable. One storyteller describes his experience of a united audience as a web of connecting strands that extend from his gut to the guts of his listeners. Another speaks of a liquid cloud that forms over the heads of the audience members. Still another says, "I can feel the audience's presence in the air; when they are with me, I can sculpt it like clay."

Whatever your perception of performing for a strongly united audience, it is a powerful experience of unity and connection.

Inviting

The next stage of relating to your audience is to *invite* them. This may happen at the moment of uniting, or it may happen later. Storyteller Jackie Torrence's smile and dramatic "Well, hello" simultaneously galvanize her listeners and invite them to listen. When I sing a song with my audience, on the other hand, they become united, but have not yet accepted an invitation to hear stories, because I have not yet invited them.

The stage of "inviting" is intangible. In the analogy of a group house tour, the "invitation" might take place outside or in the lobby, once you have gathered the group and gotten them to listen to you. You might tell them something of what could interest them inside the house, then you might walk to the stairway. If no one follows, you might make the invitation more explicit: "If you come up this stairway, I'll start by showing you the main ballroom…" or, "Is anyone ready to come in?" If no one comes at this point, you may need a showdown: "We have two choices here. I can show you the rest of the house, or I can just answer your questions while standing here." This may provoke a positive response ("Don't worry, we're coming!"), a negative response ("Let's just stay here"), or new information ("We'd love to follow you, but we can't climb stairs. Is there an elevator?").

Similarly, in a storytelling performance the invitation may be implicit, perhaps consisting of a posture, of a single word spoken with an expectant look ("Once…"), or of an introduction to your story, explaining how you learned it or why it is important to you. If that fails, you may need to make your invitation more explicit: "So, if you'll lean back and face this way, I'd like to take you on an imaginary tour of the mind of that famous villain…" In extreme cases, you may need some form of a showdown:

> It looks like you're enjoying a chance to talk to each other. At a wedding like this, it's so valuable to reconnect with relatives and friends. What I'd like to offer you for the next fifteen minutes, however, is a chance to share something all together, to hear a story about the problems of a modern relationship. Are you with me?

You can also invite while beginning your story, using nonverbal cues that say, "Are you willing to come on this journey with me?" This strategy is a little like beginning the house tour by abruptly starting to describe the house—while you walk away from your group. Your nonverbal cues (waving to them to follow, raising your eyebrows as if to say, "Are you coming?" and pausing for them to catch up with you) can make the invitation simultaneous with the spoken tour.

The audience's acceptance of your invitation may consist of a change of posture, of directing their gaze to you, or of a verbal reply, such as "Go ahead!"

RELAXED CONFIDENCE

The single most important aspect of your "invitation" to the audience is your attitude toward them.

Imagine yourself as an audience member about to hear an after-dinner speaker. If the speaker's attitude seems to be, "I'm going to knock these people dead," you will probably take a somewhat defensive posture. If the attitude is "I want to tell you how to set your life right," you may be cautiously interested, but prepared to protect yourself against a "hard sell." On the other hand, if the attitude seems more like, "I don't have much to say, and you probably don't want to hear it anyway," you will probably withhold your consent again, thinking, "I'm not sure I can trust this person to lead me anywhere."

What kind of attitude will help an audience accept a storyteller's invitation? I think of it as "relaxed confidence." If you are not confident, listeners may not be prepared to follow you—we may not accept you as a capable "helper." If, on the other hand, you are not relaxed, we may feel the need to protect ourselves from you. Your ideal attitude leaves us confident both that you will lead us and that you will not violate our boundaries. Only then are we likely to accept your invitation wholeheartedly.

If relaxed confidence is the most productive general attitude toward your audience, how do you convey it? First, you may need to deal, at least temporarily, with your own tensions and fears, as described in chapter 16: Performance Anxiety. Your audience will *not* perceive all your stage fright and feelings of inadequacy, but the looser the grip these feelings have on you, the easier it is to project relaxation and assurance. Second, pay attention to your nonverbal communication. People make unconscious interpretations of attitude less on the basis of words than on posture, facial expressions, eye contact, and tone of voice.

A general-purpose stance of relaxed confidence might include an erect but relaxed posture, relaxed hands and arms (perhaps hanging loosely at your side; definitely not tightly clasped or nervously picking lint from your clothing), and a welcoming facial expression. Of course, a posture that is considered relaxedly erect in one context will appear aggressive in a second context and timid in a third. The eye contact that suggests relaxed confidence will vary even more widely from one context to another. In performance situations in the dominant U.S. culture, for example, the storyteller who does not offer eye contact is judged as fearful or aloof; the storyteller who holds eye contact too long or too frequently with a single person is judged as invasive.

REJECTED INVITATIONS

When I fail to get my audience as a whole to accept my invitation, my story will "bomb." I may feel that some individuals are "with me" as I tell, but I will not experience the exceptional sense of unity, excitement, power, and connection that comes when I succeed. Instead of profoundly connected, I may feel profoundly alone.

When this happens, I am in a difficult situation. Personally, I am often tempted to become more dramatic, to speak louder, to make bigger gestures, to use a more emotional tone of voice—all to "get through" to my recalcitrant listeners. Only rarely is this tactic successful. Usually, it causes my uncertain audience to withdraw further from me.

Another, more effective strategy is to direct my attention to the people who *are* with me. If my first efforts fail, I can try to find another way to invite the audience. The most difficult for me—and the most effective, when I can do it—is to become vulnerable. Rather than try to "perform better," I have the option to try to become more open to them. This might take the form of speaking about my state at the moment, or even about my feelings with regard to this audience.

Or I might simply stand there with the intention of being vulnerable, trusting that my posture will communicate my openness.

My audience seems most likely to agree to follow me if I make it safe for them—in this case by showing my own struggles and feelings. In short, I can model what I want from them: to offer part of myself so that, together, we can make a journey.

Two caveats should be heeded here. First, I must remain the "helper" as I show my vulnerability; I must not make the audience feel that I expect them to become *my* helpers. Second, most of us have a tendency to emphasize some aspect of relaxed confidence at the expense of others. My personal tendency is to portray confidence (if somewhat rigidly) even when I am scared or otherwise "off;" what is missing at these moments is my relaxation, my vulnerability. For you, the missing element may be confidence, or a willingness to share what you have to say, or the expectation that your audience will have a good time or be in safe hands with you. Whatever is missing, the way to overcome a rejected invitation will usually involve resisting the urge to retreat into your habitual, more comfortable stance. Instead, you can hold out to your audience the missing element, whether it is an aspect of relaxation or an aspect of confidence.

Offering

The audience usually accepts your "invitation" by communicating to you through posture, eye contact, or facial expression. Often their acceptance is expressed gradually, through increasingly attentive listening, or through laughter and other indications of their emotional response. At first, only a few listeners may respond in this way; as your story continues, the response may spread to more and more of your audience.

At this point, you are ready to *offer* them the story. Offering differs from inviting primarily because it does not require a response from the audience. In the analogy of a house tour, offering is the stage at which you simply lead your group through each room, directing their attention toward any significant features, but allowing the group to respond to the house, not to you.

In a storytelling event, offering is an attitude, not a specific action. At this point in your performance, you usually direct more of your attention to the story and less to your audience. It may seem that images of the story begin to fill the space between you and your listeners. Or it may seem that you and the audience have entered into the world of the story, perhaps as though it were a dream. In any event, you are no longer waiting for a particular response on the part of your listeners: they have already united as an audience and accepted your invitation to receive the story.

The offering stage of your performance has an eternal quality. It can last for minutes or for hours; in some cultural contexts where events go for more than twenty-four hours, it can last for days. It will usually last until the end of your stories or until you have some other reason to change your relationship to your audience.

TOO MUCH INVITATION

The "offering" stage of the performance is usually self-sustaining. As a result, it can require the least effort from the storyteller. For some of us, however, this stage poses difficulty.

One cause of difficulty with "offering" is the unconscious continuation of the "invitation" stage. It is possible—and often a good strategy—to invite nonverbally while telling a story. But some performers continue to invite even after their invitation has been accepted.

As a listener, I sometimes feel that such performers "want something" from me, thereby distracting me from the story. The initially appropriate request for me to accept their invitation becomes annoying and inappropriate after I have already accepted it. In a house tour, it would correspond to my guide asking, "Do you want to come on the tour?" each time we entered a new room. I would want to respond, "I already told you I'm with you. Now let me see the house!"

If you are a storyteller who keeps "inviting" after it is appropriate, the solution is to break the cycle of "Oh, no, they're not with me. I'd better draw them in. They're still not with me, so I'd better draw them in more…" Usually, you will be kept in such a cycle by one of two obstacles. The first is that you expect more response to your invitation than an audience can give without being distracted from the story. In this case, you may need to change your expectations. Notice the reason you want the audience to respond so eagerly; then deal with that reason, perhaps by healing the emotional hurt that is causing you to need reassurance, or by choosing to act as though the audience is already with you.

The second possible obstacle is that you are misinterpreting the audience's signs of assent. In this case, you need to learn better what your listeners are signaling to you. Perhaps they are leaning back when you expect them to lean forward (see chapter 12). Perhaps their sour facial expressions are related to the subject matter of the story, not to their attitude toward you. Perhaps, too, their scant applause at the end of your first story was an indicator of their deep immersion, not of their lack of involvement.

Once, I gave a series of performances of "The Soul of Hope," a two-hour spiritual adventure story that makes substantial demands on my audiences. During almost every performance, I got a feeling after a few minutes that said, "Oh, no! They hate this story!" Then, at the intermission, people would come up to me saying how much they loved it. Comparing these two forms of audience response, I concluded that I was misinterpreting their signals during my performance.

I even videotaped a show—with the camera pointed at the audience. I studied the tapes (with a rehearsal buddy present) to try to learn how to interpret audience signals more correctly in the future. I was still left with the conclusion that I just did not know how to "read" the audience during this show.

Then I told a friend about this problem. She said, "Do you want to try something?" With my consent, she began acting the role of an enthusiastic, satisfied audience member raving about my show: "That was gr-r-r-r-eat! That was the best show in the world! How did you ever pull off such a great achievement?" I began to laugh. She continued for half an hour, and I continued to laugh.

After this session, I understood what had caused my difficulty. I had unconsciously been hoping that my audience would satisfy an old, unmet desire of mine for appreciation. After enough healing laughter, I was able to notice my desire and choose to put it aside.

The next performances went much better. No longer feeling unconsciously that I needed appreciation from my audience, I could stop expecting them to validate me—and therefore stop looking for a certain reaction. I could just offer them the story and relaxedly allow them to react in whatever way they desired.

Acknowledging

After I have offered a story—or a whole program of stories—to my audience, I have one more job. I must "acknowledge" them. I use this term to include several steps, including informing them that the performance is over, thanking them, letting them thank me, and finally sending them on their way.

In a traditional theatrical setting, the acknowledgment of the audience happens after the fall of the curtain. Then the applause begins, during which the audience thanks the performers. When the performers take their bows, they literally acknowledge the audience, up to now "invisible" behind the imaginary "fourth wall" of the stage. Finally, the actors retreat, the house lights go up, revealing audience members who are once again a collection of individuals instead of a group. The auditorium doors open, sending people on their way.

In an informal, conversational setting, to choose a contrasting example, "acknowledging" the audience may just consist of a look at your listeners, or perhaps a remark that signals the end of your storytelling turn, such as, "Luther here was with me when it happened! If you don't believe me, ask him." Your audience may respond with approval, by saying, "That was amazing!" or by laughing at your joke. At this point, you acknowledge their thanks, if only by asking someone else a question that might lead to a story told by a different person.

In a typical storytelling performance, the storyteller indicates that the story (or the whole program of stories) is over. This may happen through the use of a ritual ending line ("and they all lived happily ever after") or through a smile and a bow. Some storytellers use an ending formula like "and that is the story of 'The Crystal Rainbow.'" Others might say, "Thank you for listening" or "Don't forget to come next week, when we'll have..."

At this point the audience applauds, thus thanking the storyteller. Many tellers assume that they are now no longer in the helper role, but this may be a mistake since the people thanking you may be doing so within the role of beneficiary.

Imagine receiving a valued gift in the mail and being unable to thank the giver: the transaction seems incomplete until you've phoned or written your thanks. Similarly, the gift of your story is not complete until you have allowed your audience to express gratitude. You haven't finished your job as storyteller until you have accepted their thanks.

I may be uncomfortable accepting the audience's gratitude. I may feel tempted to deflect it. I may desire to express my modesty or indifference to praise. Acting on any of these impulses, however, has a negative consequence: it blocks the completion of my relationship with my listeners by preventing me from acknowledging their thanks.

Acknowledging their thanks need not be dramatic. It is usually enough to remain "present" without deflecting, minimizing, or begging for more of their thanks. In case I decide to say something, I might just reply, "You are welcome." If I wish to embellish my acknowledgment, I might indicate that my performance was mutually profitable: "This audience was so open, it was a pleasure." Or: "This story is important to me. It means a lot to know that you liked it."

Finally, I must see my audience members on their way. In most cases, all I need to do is to leave the stage or to let the next person at the table begin talking. In other cases, however, my listeners may need some information: "The next event on this festival stage will be…" Groups of children may need very specific directions: "Please stay seated until your group leader asks you to stand up, then follow that person quietly." When I perform for large groups of children, I like to play music as they leave, saying, "While your teachers lead each class out of the lunchroom, I'll play you some traveling music on my flute. Wait for your teacher to tell you to stand up!"

12

Your Effect on Your Listeners

Your effect on your listeners depends on:

- the story you choose
- your method of telling
- your relationship to your audience

To tell a story well, you need to create a common ground among these factors:

- the way you tell it
- the audience's perception of the kind of story they are hearing
- the kind of listener response you want

This chapter deals with the kinds of listener response. The most obvious distinction in audience reaction (and the most common occasion for misunderstanding) is between what I call "leaning forward" and "leaning back." You use different techniques to produce these two fundamental types of responses.

Leaning Forward

Some stories (and ways of telling) make the listener lean forward. I use the term *leaning forward* to refer to what is often a literal physical response, described by expressions such as "they were on the edge of their seats" or "they really sat up and listened." Just as often, the response may be internal only, consisting of an attitude of alertness and involvement.

Almost all humor produces the "leaning forward" response. So do most stories that rely on cleverness or irony. Such tales seem to require an alert, almost intellectual response from the audience. Listeners to these stories are using their abilities to filter, discriminate, and understand.

Listeners to a "leaning forward" story may show their involvement through their forward or erect posture, of course, but also through other physical responses such as dynamic facial expressions, active eye contact, small changes in head position that suggest alertness, sounds such as "ah," "uh-huh," and laughter, and other subtle reactions.

How do you produce such a response? Use one or more techniques that invite your listeners to be "present," alert, or focused—including humor, mental puzzles, spectacle (such as costumes, props, mime, and juggling), sudden changes in volume, voices, and position, and overt audience participation of all kinds.

Leaning Back

Other stories (and other ways of telling) make the listener lean back, relax, or "sit back and listen." When this type of story works well, you "knock them out." Your audience ends up "transported," "entranced," "lost in thought," or "carried away." This mental state may be mirrored in a relaxed or even slumped posture, or it may be shown more subtly through an inactive, "dead" or dreamy facial expression, a distant or unfocused look in the eyes (or even closed eyes), a head position that is slightly tilted back, deep breathing, very little movement, lack of vocal response, and perhaps a reluctance to interact or participate overtly.

Fairy tales often produce this *leaning back* response. Many other genres of stories may also put your audience in this kind of light trance, including epics, certain kinds of personal and religious stories, and fantasy and dreamlike stories. Fran Stallings, the pioneer writer about this kind of audience response to storytelling, believes that such a reaction often is triggered by stories that begin with a sudden loss.

I can still remember the first time I told a story that evoked this kind of response. I was a teacher in a school for "emotionally dis-turbed" children—an audience mostly of active, rebellious children who had been excluded from their local schools because of their disruptive behavior. In my first attempt at storytelling to these stu-dents, I began a Jack tale with great trepidation, mindful of this group's resistance to every activity I had tried with them. I started the traditional story:

> Well, Jack and his mother were having a hard time. So Jack had to leave home and go out in the world to make his own fortune.

At this point, I took a breath and dared a glance at the children. To my amazement, they were sitting quietly with their mouths open. No one was resisting me. No one was fighting with another student. At that moment, I fell in love with the power of stories to create the "leaning back" response.

How do you produce such a response? Stallings suggests that tra-ditional fairy-tale beginning formulas, such as "Once upon a time..." or "Once there was, there was, and yet there was not...," use nonsense or paradox for the purpose of signaling the logical part of our brains (the part that favors "leaning forward") to relin-quish control. Further, the traditional endings reverse the process by bringing us back to the present time and place, in order to signal when to end the trancelike response. Other techniques for encourag-ing "leaning back" include steadiness in voice and movement as well as a relaxed posture and reassuring demeanor.

In a given situation, it is conceivable that you might want to inter-rupt your audience's tendency to lean back, and cause them to lean forward—perhaps if you are introducing another teller or another story that will require leaning forward.

If you want listeners to continue leaning back, however, avoid interrupting this response with techniques that encourage leaning forward. Don't ask your audience to participate, don't make jokes, don't use sudden changes in loudness, pacing, or lighting, don't call attention to yourself, and don't do something that introduces your remarkable skill at something. For example, don't pull out a new musical instrument or start juggling or begin manipulating a pup-pet—although it can be fine to continue or resume such an activity that began before your audience started to "lean back." Even the use of dramatic dialogue between characters can bring your listeners forward out of trance—by introducing a device that draws their attention, or perhaps by breaking their connection to you, the narrator.

SPECIAL PROBLEMS WITH "LEANING BACK" STORIES

A very accomplished professional storyteller approached me with a problem. He had made a career of "edge of the seat" stories, specializing in humorous and clever folktales. Recently he had become fascinated with a certain fairy tale because of its impact on him as a listener. When he tried to perform it, however, he felt that the story "wasn't working; it fell flat."

When I asked him how he knew that the story wasn't working, he said, "Well, it's strange. After I perform that story, some people always tell me they loved the story. But I just don't feel that the audience is with me." Then he went on to describe the audience's response during his tellings—which was exactly the "leaning back" response outlined here.

The problem was not with his telling or with the audience's reaction. The problem was with his interpretation of their reaction. After years of "leaning forward" responses, he interpreted "leaning back" as a negative thing. In fact, before coming to me for coaching, he had experimented with adding humor, satire, and participation to the story—ways to get the kind of response he was accustomed to. But that "didn't work with this story," because they disturbed his listeners, as he correctly sensed. What he did not understand was that they conflicted with the audience's desire to lean back and enjoy the story.

The "leaning back" story requires a great deal of trust. First, the audience must trust the storyteller enough to enter this light form of trance, which one storyteller has likened to a shamanic journey. Your listeners may, in fact, be journeying deep into their unconscious minds. Second, once rapport has been created and the audience begins to "lean back," a storyteller must trust that people are following him or her on this internal, dreamlike journey.

Some Genre-Related Effects on Your Audience

The moment you say, "Did you hear the one about...," your listeners anticipate a joke and begin to "lean forward." They also prepare themselves for an anticipated punch line. In general, the moment you indicate the genre of a story, you generate a sense of expectations in your audience—including a set of likely responses.

What people will expect, of course, depends on their relationships to you, to fellow listeners, and to jokes in general. They may be eager to laugh, or they may take the attitude that says, "I dare you to try to make me laugh!" They may be hoping for the titillation of an off-color joke, or they may be bracing themselves for subject matter of which they disapprove.

Although you will probably prefer a friendly and positive reaction to the genre of your story, it is possible to *seek* listeners' attitudes, including the apparently negative ones. Some traditional jokes and riddles, for example, were developed to make use of listeners' disapproving attitudes toward sexual or scatological jokes or riddles. They describe a situation indirectly in a way that suggests off-color content; then, when the listener jumps to the indicated conclusion and begins to appear uncomfortable, the joke ends innocently. The humorous effect depends on the contrast between what the listener is led to expect and what the storyteller actually says.

Some genres, such as formula tales and certain kinds of sermons, make special use of repetition that intensifies audience reactions, and may even create a sense of timelessness.

Scary stories depend on a balance between fear and safety. On the one hand, the danger in a scary story needs to be experienced as genuinely frightening. On the other, the danger needs to be remote enough that your listeners are not too frightened to enjoy listening. When telling scary stories to adults, your challenge in creating this balance is usually to make the danger credible. Thus, a favorite genre of scary stories for adults is the "urban legend," which mimics the reality of the personal experience story. When telling to children, however, your challenge may be to keep the story from becoming *too* frightening. If you overuse the effective ploys of realism associated with this genre (such as the confederate who creates spine-chilling sound just outside the window), you may find your audience restoring the balance by interrupting the story for assurance ("Is that real?") or by "fighting" you (saying perhaps "You're making that sound with your foot!" or "That doesn't scare me!").

A Response to Personal Experience Stories

A particularly important response to genre occurs in the case of certain personal experience stories. Whenever you tell of an upsetting experience as though it happened to you, your listeners will, to some degree, react with sympathy and concern. This is a usual response to the conversational genres of "upsetting personal experiences."

In a performance situation, however, you may want to tell a story that did not happen to you personally, as though it did. If your audience interprets the genre as a genuine personal experience story, they may be angered to learn later that the story is fictional or happened to someone else. The effect of the personal experience genre is so strong that I have seen outraged audiences who were warned in advance that a story was fictional, but who were so convinced by the storytellers effective, nonverbal suggestion that the story was true, that they forgot what they were told.

In such situations, you may want to weaken the signals that say, "This happened to me." You might tell the story in the third person, use theatrical lighting, add a piece of costume when you tell the story, or change your posture or voice (to suggest, "I am speaking the words of someone else").

Alternatively, you can make the "disclaimer" dramatic enough to be remembered. For instance, you can create a prologue describing the person to whom the story happened. By making the prologue vivid (and perhaps even returning to it at the end of your story), you ensure that it will not be forgotten. This classic literary device is used in numerous short stories and even in narrative poems such as the "Rhyme of the Ancient Mariner"—in which the narrator describes the disheveled old man who then tells his story in the first person. Another way to highlight your disclaimer is to add a joke or some other piece of memorable language to your statement that the story didn't happen to you: "Everything I am about to say is true— or my name isn't Mortimer J. Snodgrass."

13

PROGRAM PLANNING

In the beginning of my storytelling career, when I knew only one story, program planning was easy! Later, I knew three stories for adult audiences. One was fifteen minutes long, one was seven minutes, and the third lasted three minutes. At this stage, program planning became a matter of arithmetic: "Let's see…they want me for twenty minutes, so fifteen plus three is eighteen, with two minutes for introductions and transitions."

Still later, when I had ten or fifteen (or more) stories in my repertory, I started creating detailed program-lists for each performance. I would think, "I'll start with something short and lively for this group of preschoolers, like the movement song, 'Everyone is Different.' Then I'll give them a short, participatory story like 'I'm Not Sleepy Yet'…" After I had listed each item in my program, I would create clever transitions between them: "How can I go from the movement song to the story? I know: I can say, 'Yep, we're different even in the way we sleep. Some of us need a lot of help to feel safe at night, and here's a story about a little boy who had a terrible time feeling safe enough to go to sleep.'"

Such transitions can be very useful. They carefully direct the thread of the audience's attention from one subject to the next. They create a sense that the program is a whole, tied neatly together.

At the same time, these transitions can have drawbacks. As clever as they may be, they are generally less interesting than the actual stories, and they use time that might better be spent going directly to the next interesting image. Also, the sense of unity they create can be misleading, since they are often based on superficial similarities between stories rather than on a unifying principle for a program.

Nowadays, my personal preference is for two forms of transitions. The first—and most common—is simply to jump to the next story. I find that a clean and sudden leap into a new story often creates a sense of drama that grabs the audience's attention. The second is to create transitions based on the MIT (the Most Important Thing) not of the individual story, but of the program as a whole.

The MIT for a Program

I am often called on to perform stories (and songs) on a particular subject for children. Over the years, I have created programs on more than fifty topics, from Animals to Colonial History to Teddy Bears. I have learned that a key step in creating—and performing—such programs is to ask myself, "What is the main thing I want to say about this subject?" The answer to this question is the MIT (Most Important Thing) about the program.

For example, I created a program about "Freedom." Of course, this is an enormous subject, so I had no choice but to narrow it in some way. What way? The main thing I wanted to say about freedom, I discovered, was that no one can be truly free until everyone is free. Thus, true freedom is not achievable by an individual, but only by a society. Starting with this idea, I found several stories that supported it. One Jewish legend connected several scenes in the story of Moses and the Exodus to this very theme. Another story from West Africa described how all the small animals in a region cooperated to bring freedom to their entire valley. These two stories together lasted about twenty minutes. To complete a thirty-minute program, I found and adapted two songs that fit my MIT for the program.

Now I had a program that fit together around a single aspect of the subject of freedom. One of my two songs contained an explicit statement of my theme. I decided that I needed no transitions; at the end of each story or song, I just began the next, trusting that the four different statements of the same theme would make it clear.

I was called on years later for a longer program about freedom, this time for a setting where I wanted to emphasize a second theme: the idea that the freedom of a society is the responsibility of each person. Once I found a story about this aspect of freedom, I realized that my Jewish and African stories also supported it, if only to establish a necessary premise for my new MIT. I now had two ideas to relate with three stories. In this case, I decided to use verbal transitions to state the relationship of my two ideas to each other.

Thus, my decision about transitions used in performance is largely a result of my choice of MIT for the program as a whole. When I change the MIT, I make a different decision about the transitions.

Planning by the Slots

As I gained experience developing and performing programs for young children or families, I noticed that I tended to use four or five different kinds of items, no matter what exact stories and songs I performed. In other words, my programs had an underlying structure, which was determined by the typical needs of my young listeners. In most cases, a thirty-to-forty-minute program contained four or five items:

1. an opening, participatory song
2. a short, participatory story
3. a "stand up and stretch" song or story
4. a longer, "leaning back" story
5. (optional) a final, lively song or story including on-stage participation by volunteers from the audience

These "slots" in a program work for me with most audiences that contain a sizable number of young children; you may find other kinds of slots evolving from your work. But if you know to look for this kind of structure, it may free your program planning.

Now, rather than plan an exact program, I most often just make a list of candidates for each slot. Thus, I list three or four participatory songs that might serve to open my program. I list all my short, participatory stories that might work with the exact age group in question, etc. Then I choose one from each list at the exact moment of performance.

Why would I want to leave so many decisions to make during my actual shows? Because I had found a new principle for program planning: my unconscious "radar" for finding just the right story for a given group.

Unbidden Images

In 1982 I attended the National Storytelling Festival in Jonesborough, Tennessee. One of the performers, Ron Evans of Saskatchewan, Canada, did something that startled me. He stood up for his turn in a three-teller program and said something like, "As a keeper of the sacred stories of my tribal tradition, I only tell stories that call to me to be told. At this moment, no story is calling to me. Therefore, I will not tell a story at this time." Then he sat back down without performing.

I remember thinking, "This Ron Evans has a high level of integrity about telling his stories, an integrity that I can scarcely imagine." I had never experienced *one* story "calling to me," much less all the stories I told.

By the time I knew about forty or fifty stories, I was much more facile in creating programs, but I was developing a new problem: stray images. I'd arrive at a performance with my carefully crafted list of stories to tell. As I watched the audience arrive, I would sometimes find myself imagining scenes from stories that I knew but that were not on my list. These images came to me spontaneously. Since they weren't from stories I planned to tell, I'd suppress them. What an annoyance they were!

Then, one day, I was to perform in the late afternoon for the staff of a private, secular school. I had spent the school day performing for the children in each classroom. Now, as I watched the staff arrive and interact, an image came to me from a story I had not planned to tell. Feeling especially confident and experimental that day, I decided to make room for the unplanned story in my program. After the performance, two or three people sought me out to say, "You don't know what we've been through as a staff, but that one story was exactly what we needed to hear. Thank you."

Was this what it meant to have a story "call to me"? I'd have to try to trust the "stray images," and notice if they guided me to stories that my audience actually would benefit from hearing.

For the next year, nearly every time that I had the nerve to tell a story which had beckoned in this way to be told, someone would come up to me afterwards and say something like, "Thank you for that story. It seemed as if it was meant for me." I began to feel more confident about changing my plans when an image from a story came into my mind.

One Friday I arrived at a synagogue. I was nervous because I was beginning an entire weekend in residence. I had never told so many stories to the same community before. I spent Friday afternoon talking to the rabbi and his wife about the needs of the congregation for the weekend. I mapped out what stories I might tell, including a seven-minute Hasidic story for services that evening.

When I stood up during services to tell my story, I took a moment to prepare myself, as I always do. I imagined the "moment of triumph" of the story, reminding myself of its emotional flavor. Then I imagined the opening scene of the story. That night, I saw it exceptionally clearly: an old woman was walking toward the Baal Shem Tov (the legendary founder of the Hasidic movement) begging once again to be granted a son. The Baal Shem Tov was about to tell her that she could have a son, but that the boy's soul was a very old soul, and could stay on earth with her only for a short while. As soon as I had seen the opening scene in my mind, I began to describe it to the audience—I began to tell the tale.

Ten minutes into my story, nearing a crucial moment in the plot, I suddenly realized: this was not the seven-minute story I had meant to tell! What had gone wrong? Thinking back in panic, I remembered that I had imagined the triumph of the correct story. But when I had shifted to the opening scene, I had seen the opening scene of an entirely different story about the Baal Shem Tov. What was that old woman doing in this story? Her story takes fifteen minutes to tell, and all I could do now was finish it. As I returned to my seat, I heard one of the older members of the congregation whisper, "That was so *long!*" His wife said, "Shhh!"

When I returned to the rabbi's house, he began telling me about the arrangements for my performance the next morning. I interrupted him, saying, "Something happened tonight that shook me up. I can't concentrate until I tell you about it."

He paused while I told him about telling the wrong story—against my will. "The most disturbing thing," I said, "is that, usually, when a story comes to me that strongly, at least someone in the audience comes up to me later to say that they needed it. But tonight, even though the whole congregation shook my hand and thanked me as they left, no one said, 'That story was for me.'"

The rabbi suddenly looked uncomfortable. He looked at the floor. After a moment, he said, "It was me." Looking up, he went on slowly. "You see, our son died a few years ago...I've never really accepted it. That was the story that *I* needed to hear."

At that moment, I vowed to remain open to stories that called to me. Therefore, I prefer to plan in a way that will always keep a story at hand, so that I am not caught without a story to tell—but that always gives me a chance to say, "What story is calling to me now?"

14

Developing Audiences for Your Needs

Usually, I find myself hired to tell stories to a particular audience. As a result, I am usually in the role of reacting to the needs of a pre-existing audience. But I can also be the one to seek audiences in order to meet my own needs as a storyteller.

In chapter 6: Learning the Story, I advocate telling to live audiences as a key tool for developing stories. But what if the audiences I need don't happen along when I need them?

I can develop audiences for myself. And I can make sure I have the appropriate kinds of audiences for the various stages of my developing stories.

The Rehearsal Buddy

The foundation of my support system of audiences is my network of rehearsal buddies. These peer coaches agree to listen to my stories one-on-one in return for my attention on some task of their own.

During my turn in a rehearsal-buddy session, I am the beneficiary. Therefore, I can tell a story at any level of preparedness, from "talking about" the story, to telling fragments of it, to performing it from start to end. In these settings, no story is too raw to be worked on.

No matter what other practice audiences I have, I always have a need for this least demanding of all audiences. In addition, because these sessions require only two of us and a place to work together, they are relatively easy to schedule and to make a regular part of my life.

The value of a rehearsal buddy is similar to the value of a paid coach. The paid coach, of course, is reimbursed with money rather than attention. Depending on your situation, it may make sense to use a paid coach in place of a rehearsal buddy. For most of us, however, the coach supplements the rehearsal buddy. We may consult the paid coach to get us started on a story before continuing with our rehearsal buddies. Or we may use a paid coach *after* working with our rehearsal buddies, to give us a professional point of view on our "finished product" or to help with any stuck places that remain.

The Home Audience

My time during a rehearsal buddy session is entirely for me; I am the beneficiary. To move from telling a story as beneficiary to telling it as helper, it's good to have "intermediate" audiences who expect to be the beneficiaries, but who are willing to be my helpers for a short time if I need it.

The most important audience for developing storytellers is usually what I call a "home audience," people available on a regular basis. They are listeners who can become safe enough that I can try out stories which won't always work well. I can get to know them so well that I can gauge a new story by their reaction to it.

Sometimes, such an audience is literally in the home, as in the community of friends and relatives that forms the audience for many traditional tellers. Theatrical storyteller Jay O'Callahan also found an audience in his home; he began telling to his two young children. Day after day, he would tell them impromptu stories while doing chores, in the bathtub, and at bedtime. He told the stories for the joy of telling them, but occasionally a story—perhaps one in twenty—would be worth writing down and remembering. Later, when he began performing professionally, he would continue to try out his new creations on Ted and Laura—whose reactions to stories were so familiar to Jay that he could depend on them for reliable feedback.

Other "home audiences" are outside the home. Sid Lieberman told to his high school English classes. Jackie Torrence told to the patrons at the library where she worked. Donald Davis told first to his extended family and then to the congregation to whom he ministered. Brother Blue developed as a storyteller by telling on the streets of Cambridge, Massachusetts—to an audience that was different every day, but fundamentally similar in composition.

After Jay O'Callahan's children grew up, he felt the lack of his home audience. In response, he began inviting friends and neighbors to his office for regular "practice tellings." Over time, he has developed a new community of interested story listeners, many of whom are devoted to hearing his works in progress.

The home audience helps a teller develop repertory and style. Such listeners will let you tell tales that flop, but are still pleased to hear you tell. Because you grow very familiar with their responses, they become a weather vane for the condition of any story you tell them.

Other Practice Audiences

What other kinds of audiences do you need—besides rehearsal buddies and a "home audience"—in order to develop your stories? This depends on the kind of situations in which you will finally perform.

If you plan to tell to small groups of school children, you will probably need a "home audience" of at least one group of school children (classroom teachers have a great advantage here), plus access to a few more groups. These other groups will be the trial audiences for stories you have already told to your home audience and are now ready to try out on others. Before you tell a story in a paid setting, you probably will want to tell it a few times to different trial audiences.

If, on the other hand, you want to tell in a setting that demands a high degree of polish, such as a regional or national festival or for a theatrical audition, you will need even more kinds of trial audiences.

One year, I decided to invite newspaper reviewers to a six-performance run of a show for adults I called "Milk from the Bull's Horn: Tales of Nurturing Men." I certainly didn't want to have reviewers present until the show was seasoned. Therefore, I committed to the run almost a year in advance, then prepared a rough schedule of practice performances.

Working backwards from the desired May performance date, I realized that I would need several audiences for whom I could perform the entire show in the month or two before the run. But in order to have the entire show ready to try out with audiences in March and April, I would need earlier chances to work on one act at a time starting *this* September. Since I was making these rough plans in July, I had little time to lose! I had to find trial listeners.

Who would be my practice audiences? I used a combination of existing and new listeners. My existing listeners included my rehearsal buddies, of course, but also the monthly story-sharing sessions in the Boston area, where I could tell at most a twenty-minute segment of my show. Others were my storytelling classes (in some of them I could tell for as long as an hour if I did it during an appropriate lesson) and public "story swaps" that were part of local concerts and festivals.

I planned to augment these existing practice audiences with new ones. I would schedule some "house concerts," by inviting friends over for an evening performance at my home or at the home of a friend. I would also seek out some existing groups to tell stories to. Because the subject of my show seemed that it would appeal to those working in the "men's movement," I contacted various associations and volunteered to perform the show free—if they could schedule it in one of the months when I needed audiences.

I became alert for new audience possibilities. Whenever an organization approached me about performing for them, I considered whether they might make an appropriate practice audience. If they wanted me to perform for them but could not afford my fee, I might say,

> I'm sorry you can't afford the program you asked about. But between November and May, I'm working on a new story. If you'd let me try it out on you during that time, I'd perform for less than my usual fee.

Knowing what I needed in the way of trial listeners and when I would need them, I was able to convert several interactions from

"Sorry, I can't help you" into "Actually, we can help each other." One of these groups even offered to have me return any time I needed to practice, and so became part of my permanent network of practice audiences.

A BALANCED DIET OF AUDIENCES

The number and kind of practice audiences you need depends on the type of storytelling you do. In particular, it depends on how demanding your regular audiences are and how often you perform for them.

If you tell only to the second-grade classroom you teach, the audience probably does not expect a great deal of polish—but your students might demand a large, frequently expanding repertory of stories. In other words, you may need to develop stories frequently, but not necessarily impeccably. You may have little use for opportunities to tell in a very demanding setting, except perhaps to aid your overall growth as a storyteller.

If, on the other hand, you perform only for large assemblies of second-graders in one school after another, you may get by with fewer stories (because you rarely tell to the same audience a second time), but your stories must be foolproof. One "bomb" could leave you the unenviable task of restoring order to a cafeteria filled with three hundred unruly children. In other words, you may need to develop stories infrequently, but to a high degree of polish and predictability. Once you have developed a reliable set, you may have little incentive to add new ones beyond the need to keep your art from becoming stale. Since the external demands do not require new material, you will need to set up a series of practice performances that force you to take new pieces through the steps by which you once perfected your tried-and-true stories.

Whatever your exact needs for listeners, you can find a way to meet them. Part of your responsibility to yourself as a storyteller is to take charge of developing the audiences that will meet your needs as a teller.

Your Relationship to Your Self

Storytelling is easy.
Storytelling is physically demanding.
Storytelling is emotionally demanding.

All three of the above statements are true. Storytelling is, after all, a natural and universal human activity so commonly a part of human interaction that it is frequently unrecognized except when put on a concert stage.

At the same time, the storyteller, like the actor or the clown, uses the physical instruments of body and voice. The better conditioned the instruments, the better the possible results.

Finally, storytelling provides little physical or emotional protection from the audience: little or no lighting, sets, costuming, make-up, or props; no theatrical "fourth wall;" no other players to share the blame or the fame. The storyteller stands vulnerable and alone between the audience and the story, every shortcoming as noticeable and potentially as troubling as a dark smudge on a crystal window-pane.

Storytelling is easy. But reaching its highest level requires you to develop your body, your voice, your psyche, and your support team. In short, it requires you to develop your relationship to your self.

15
YOUR VOICE

People can tell stories well with a voice that is damaged by stress or limited by disability—or even without a voice at all. Some of our great contemporary storytellers use American Sign Language. Famed physicist Stephen Hawking captivates lecture audiences with a mechanical "voice."

Yet, for most of us, voice is our most important tool as a storyteller. All other things being equal, maintaining ease and flexibility in your voice helps you be the best storyteller you can be. A well-cared for voice maintains vocal ease and flexibility, helping you to achieve maximum expressiveness and cut fatigue. Further, it helps you avoid the eventual harm that fatigue can bring to the delicate parts of your vocal apparatus.

In its essence, using your voice is easy. To be sure, it takes most of us many years to discover the easy use of our voice—which is not to say that "voice takes years of work." We *can* say, "It may take years to learn how to stop working at voice."

Reducing Tension

The key obstacle to vocal ease is unnecessary tension. If your voice has such tension, it's because you are putting unproductive effort into it. First, you can use physical means to reduce tension. Then you can discover your unproductive effort (which is usually unconscious) and redirect it in more effective ways.

THE HEALING YAWN

Fortunately, our bodies have a built-in mechanism for reducing physical tension: the yawn. I believe that yawning assists in the healing of some forms of physical distress. The yawn appears to increase the supply of oxygen to certain tissues. Voice teachers and other speech professionals have long applauded its relaxing effects on the muscles of the mouth and throat.

A speech pathologist told me of her first experience with the healing power of the yawn. During her internship as a speech pathologist, she was asked to treat a woman with severely inflamed vocal cords. Examining the woman, she found no likely cause for the inflammation except muscular tension. Newly interested in the function of the yawn, the intern asked the woman how much she yawned. She was amazed by the answer: "Never."

Pursuing this combination of unexplained tension with the absence of yawning, the speech pathologist tried to teach the woman to yawn. She explained the value of yawning for relieving vocal tension. She began to yawn directly at the woman. In time, the pathologist succeeded in getting the woman to yawn back. After several sessions reinforcing this new practice of yawning, the woman's symptoms disappeared!

If yawning is so good for us, why is it prohibited in polite company?

First, we associate yawning with boredom. Boredom is lack of stimulation. When we have inadequate physical movement, our bodies apparently increase circulation (and decrease tension) in our unmoving muscles by yawning. Thus, yawns actually counteract some effects of boredom. By association, however, yawning is seen as a *statement* of boredom.

Second, in a society that values "productivity" above physical well-being, virtually all of us have a back-log of tension waiting to be dispelled by yawns. We stifle our yawns so thoroughly (and maintain so much physical tension) that only when nearing sleep are we relaxed and unguarded enough to allow ourselves to yawn. As a result, we associate yawning with being sleepy.

Taken together, these factors make yawning appear to be an insulting statement of lack of interest.

The contagion of yawning—used so effectively by the speech pathologist—also contributes to our social sanctions. Someone else's yawn "reminds" our body to yawn. And since we tend to resent anything that disturbs our concentration on our current task, we view a nearby yawn as a rude imposition.

In a society that needs to yawn but doesn't, we expend effort suppressing this natural way to relieve tension. The less we yawn, the greater our tension and the more we need to yawn.

Like everyone in our society, you will have to deal with the general prohibition against yawns. Knowing that tension is the main obstacle to easy use of your voice, however, and that yawning is a mechanism for relieving vocal tension, you can try to find ways to help maintain your voice through abundant yawning. And you can be sure to incorporate yawning into your preparation before you tell a story.

THE SOURCES OF TENSION

As babies, we come straight out of the womb with the ability to project our voices clearly, at high volume, for hours at a time. But in the years that follow, we add tensions—habitual muscular efforts—that interfere with our relaxed vocal power. (Any tensed muscle will affect our voice directly if it restricts our breathing, our airway, our vocal cords, or our mouth and tongue; other muscle tensions can require compensating tensions that end up affecting our voice indirectly.)

We add these tensions in order to accomplish specific effects. For example, we might learn to avoid censure by sounding inoffensive, to avoid victimization by sounding dangerous, or to get the attention of a preoccupied caretaker by sounding desperate, wheedling, or commanding.

We may add physical tensions to change our appearance. We learn to stand in a way that maximizes the positive attention directed at us while minimizing the negative attention. Depending on our surroundings and temperament, this may mean stiffening our stomach, sucking it in, or letting it sag. We may learn to keep our head down to avoid challenging those in authority, or to stick our head forward to warn challengers away.

Still other tensions serve the function of regulating feelings. In a situation where it is labeled as "babyish" to cry, we may discover that we can prevent tears by keeping our breathing shallow. Where it is "sissy" to tremble with fear, we may learn to tense the muscles of our upper abdomen. Where our righteous anger might bring reprisals, we may learn to "clamp ourselves down" with our neck and shoulder muscles. Each of these tensions will affect our voice.

We may, of course, also add some form of effort in response to incorrect or misunderstood instruction in the use of our voice. Someone may have told us to "open our jaw wide," for example, and we may be doing so—not in a relaxed way, but in a way that also draws our jaw backward. I spent years tensing my stomach in an unproductive way because of incorrect instructions given during wind-instrument lessons.

Some efforts we apply all the time; others we only apply in certain situations. A number of people use their voices well until they begin to perform; then they distort their voices in a way that reflects a misunderstanding of what performing is.

Occasionally, too, we change our voices for strictly internal reasons. If you are ticklishly sensitive to the buzzing sensation caused by your full voice, for example, you may learn to speak softly enough that your head cavity will not vibrate. If, on the other hand, you feel comforted by the internal massage your voice can give to your nose, chin, or throat, you may choose to direct your voice to your own body, not to your listeners.

All these unconscious strategies (and countless others) deserve to be thought of as a brilliant solution to a given situation. They are to be celebrated. They were creative responses.

The problem with such strategies, however, is that they become habitual. After a time, we don't even realize that we are applying effort. Therefore, we have no idea how to stop.

WHAT ARE YOU TRYING TO DO?

To regain ease of vocal production, try to discover what efforts you are making, then discover why you make them, and finally substitute a new intention. For clues about your unconscious efforts, ask yourself, "How do I feel before (as) (after) I tell a story?" If you realize you feel afraid, ask, "What do I feel afraid of?" For other clues, ask yourself, "How do I feel when I succeed?" or "How do I feel when it does not go well?" Notice whatever goes through your mind in answer to these questions.

If you are afraid of being humiliated, or of being exposed as an impostor, or of being ignored, these feelings may be causing you to apply effort. You may be trying to protect yourself from humiliation, or to prove that you know what you are talking about, or to make sure that you are finally heard.

Alternatively, get direct feedback on your voice or posture. For example, you might listen to yourself on tape, or ask a trusted friend to listen to you. Ask, "What is the effect of the voice you hear? What does this person seem to want? If you couldn't understand the words, what would be the message of the voice alone?" A good voice teacher or body worker can help here, of course, by noticing your tensions, then helping you experience them consciously.

CHANGING THE DECISION

Once you have discovered an effort you are applying, you need to learn your motivation for applying it. If you don't learn and rescind your original motivation, you may find yourself putting effort into omitting the effort!

The efficient way to stop applying effort is to rescind your decision to apply it in the first place. First, celebrate your original decision to apply the effort. Notice how, given all the circumstances that surrounded you, it once served you well.

Next, note that your reason for applying the effort no longer exists. Look around you when you are telling stories. Is there anyone actually trying to usurp you or diminish you? Probably not. Therefore, your successful strategy from the past is no longer needed.

Instead of sticking out your chin, for example, try to notice that the listeners are your friends and want to hear your story. If you are in fact safe, then a relaxed, confident posture is warranted. As you relax, you may feel fear. Your body is getting the message that it is finally safe to heal its stored-up fear.

Once you have rescinded your original decision to create a tension, find a way to apply your effort more effectively. For example, focus on your intention in telling the story: what you love about it, what you want to communicate through it, or the gift you want your audience to receive from it.

I used to have great difficulties performing in large spaces, until one day I began a five-day engagement featuring four half-hour shows in the passageways of a museum. By the end of the first day, nearly voiceless, I realized that I could not physically repeat what I had just done. I needed to change my concept of the task or of how to accomplish it.

The next day, faced with my amorphous crowd and the milling visitors beyond them, I thought, "What am I trying to do?" At that moment, I realized that I had been straining to reach everyone I could see. Instead, I decided, I would imagine how much of the space I could fill with my voice, and then I would speak only to the people within it. It worked! I left the museum the second day with a tired but still-functional voice. And I had learned that I can redefine a vocal task in a way that allows success.

Special Problems in Teaching Voice

Because vocal tensions usually come from decisions that are unconscious, we need other people who can notice what we cannot. But getting good help with voice can be tricky, for three basic reasons.

First, voice is so simple that it's difficult to teach. It would be easier to teach someone how to perform a conscious act than how *not* to perform an *un*conscious act. As a result, teaching voice demands rare skills. The teacher must be able to notice your habitual effort, then help you notice it. The teacher also needs to find a way to help you direct your efforts productively.

Such teaching skills may be rare in any field. But teaching voice poses a second challenge. Because our ears are built into the same body that produces our voice, we can't hear ourselves as others do. This tempts the teacher to say, "There! That just sounded good! Do what you just did and you'll be fine."

With a voice teacher who is good enough to recognize effective vocal production—but not good enough to help us experience it internally—we may end up with a mechanical series of things to concentrate on. This may actually result in good vocal production, but at a great cost. Much of our attention becomes tied up in producing sound as vocal mechanics become separated from artistic intentions. Our voice may sound good and last long, but still lack full connection to our storytelling impulse.

All too often, however, we do not even end up with good vocal production. We just add a list of conscious instructions ("Breathe from the diaphragm," "Keep the soft palate raised") to our existing list of unconscious instructions ("Keep your stomach flat," "Bite down on your anger"). The result is conflicting tensions, not lack of tension.

The third problem in teaching voice is cultural. People in different cultures prefer different vocal qualities, sometimes including various forms of constriction and effort. This is clearest in the case of singing, where the vocal qualities praised in country music are obviously different from those sought in opera or in Japanese Noh theater. But similar considerations apply to spoken voices, as well. For example, think of your own stereotypes of various cultural groups whose speech sounds "shrill," "melodious," "flat," or "dramatic" to you. To them, of course, your group doubtless sounds the opposite.

If all voice teachers were trained to help storytellers achieve whatever vocal qualities they wanted, cultural variety would not cause a problem. Some voice teachers are, in fact, trained to take their goals from their students, but such teachers are still relatively uncommon. The difficulty arises because most voice teachers are trained to prefer the vocal qualities valued in "classical" music (Western European-based art music) or in "cultured" theater (also a Western European-based form). As a result, they often present two kinds of strivings as though there were no difference between them: eliminating individual vocal difficulties and eliminating culturally derived patterns. This confusion often creates conflicts (usually unconscious ones) and impedes progress.

Do you need help with your voice? Almost everyone who tells stories extensively will benefit from at least occasional help with habitual tensions. In the more extreme cases, if you are experiencing warning signs such as customary hoarseness or laryngeal pain, you need immediate help to prevent long-lasting damage.

Who should help you? There are many skilled and helpful voice professionals. Because of the three pitfalls of vocal instruction just mentioned, you will need to be thoughtful as you decide which helper you hire. Ask for recommendations from those in your area, and, whenever practical, interview a potential helper before signing up and interview several potential helpers before choosing one.

Once you have begun, give your helper credit for hearing what you cannot hear, but do not give up your inner sense of what is actually helpful to you.

Vocal Warm-Up

Any time I prepare to tell a story that is more than a few minutes long, or to a large audience, or in any situation which makes me anxious, I find that I need to warm up my voice. Just as a runner cannot go from rest to full speed without warming up, a speaker can rarely perform well without taking some time to "tune up" the breathing apparatus, the muscles of the neck, throat and tongue, and the resonant cavities of the head.

There are as many successful ways to warm up as there are performers. In time, you will develop your own routine, and the ability to change it to meet the unique needs of your storytelling situation and your physical and emotional state. What follows is my own personal warm-up; use it to inspire your own.

First I loosen up physically, gently stretching my neck, back, calves, and thighs. Then I check for tension in my throat; I use both hands to gently move my whole voice box from side to side. To loosen my jaw, I open it wide, then ease it to one side and to the other. I stick out my tongue a few times. Then I massage my jaw muscles, coaxing them to relax.

Next, I take a few deep breaths, trying to enjoy the luxury of filling my lungs completely at my own pace. Then I make my first sound, a gentle yawning (something like a sigh) that starts at a comfortable middle pitch and descends. If this stimulates real yawns, I take it as a sign of appropriate relaxation. If necessary, I spend several minutes yawning until no more yawns want to come.

Now I begin to hum softly, "Nnnh…" I try to feel the sound resonating in my head cavities. After a few single-pitch hums, I try a little three-note tune: do-re-mi-re-do, sung, "Nnnh, nnnh, nnnh, nnnh, nnnh, nnnh." As I sing this softly a few times, I check for relaxation in my throat, mouth, and tongue, and for a buzzing resonance throughout my head. I usually feel the buzzing more on one side of my head than on the other, so I try to spread it to the rest of my head, usually by imagining a kind of relaxing or opening of my head cavities. Then I try to feel the buzzing in and around my nose, then up in the intersection of my nose and brows. I know I've succeeded at the slightly nebulous task of opening all the relevant cavities when I feel my entire head resonating. It is an enjoyable feeling of wholeness, a kind of internal massage.

Now I sing my three-note hum-song again and again, each time a half-step higher. I aim for relaxation, openness, and head-buzz. If I feel or hear constriction, I repeat the "song" at the same pitch, trying to relax my mouth and throat until the constriction is gone. As I repeat the song at different pitches, I try raising my arms to the sides, to experience an open rib cage. Other times, I try standing on one leg while raising the other knee in front of me, to experience singing with my abdominal muscles activated. Still other times, I lean my head against a wall, supporting my angled body with my neck muscles as I sing, to experience singing with altered neck tension and head position. When I have reached my highest comfortable pitch, I stop. Then I go back to a middle pitch and repeat the process, this time starting the "song" a half-step lower each time. When I reach my lowest comfortable pitch, I stop.

At some point in a warm-up, most people practice vowel sounds (and perhaps also consonants) separately or in series, perhaps in the form "Ma, me, mi, mo, mu." I find that, for some reason, this method is ineffective for me. Instead, I "activate" the vowels and consonants by singing a song that I know well and have had many pleasant experiences singing. This stage in my warm-up is the first time that I focus on "projecting" a sound or imagine communicating with my voice. If I hear or feel tension at any particular pitch as I sing, I go back to my hum-song for that pitch, perhaps adding my arm-lift, leg-lift, or neck-lean. Or, depending on the location of the tension, I might take another moment to loosen my throat or massage my jaw muscles.

Finally, I practice any difficult vocal sections of the stories I am likely to tell. If there are songs, I begin with them, paying special attention to portions of them that are difficult for me. For example, I might sing a phrase that has a difficult leap in it, trying to imagine fully the feeling and sound of that leap so that it won't catch me unprepared.

After going over the songs, I take some time with any characters who have special voices and with any spoken lines that might be difficult. For example, in one show there is a scene in which a character despairs. Naturally, at this point I lower the loudness of my voice to reflect his diminishing energy. Unfortunately, I tend to reduce the volume until the audience can no longer hear me. To counter this, I try to convey the feeling of the character's lack of energy without too great a reduction in volume. By reminding myself before the show what this feels like, I increase the likelihood that I will succeed at doing it.

That is my personal routine when I have five or ten minutes (or more) to warm up. When I have less time (or when time has passed between my warm-up and my performance), I focus on a few key areas: tension in my throat (gently moving my voice box side to side), taking deep breaths, humming to feel the resonance in my head. When I have even less time, I try at least to take some deep breaths. If I am sitting in public waiting to perform (and therefore can't make noise), I will try to yawn unobtrusively. To experience breathing as it occurs when speaking, I exhale while hissing quietly; this provides some of the air resistance that is normally provided by my vibrating vocal cords.

If my time is so limited that I cannot warm up as fully as I need to, I try to incorporate my final warm-up into the beginning of my performance. I begin with a song that I know well and perform easily, or I pay special attention to my breathing and muscular relaxation during the first few minutes. Some tellers have created clever beginnings to their performances that actually include their needed warm-up. If you are caught without time to warm up, you can always begin, "Do you know how a storyteller warms up? First, I give a yawn. Try it with me…"

The key to warming up is to be gentle and to focus on the experience of breathing, of resonance, and of articulating speech sounds. My warm-up is a time to enjoy my body and my voice while preparing it for the enjoyable performance to come.

Like warming up, using your voice in general is easy. You need only remove the tensions you have learned to apply. Then, you can allow your power—both vocal and artistic—to flow.

16

PERFORMANCE ANXIETY

There is good news about fear. Here are the headlines:

- Half of what we call performance anxiety is useful, and the other half has no relationship to reality.

- Even the irrational part can be diminished with some long-term work.

- No matter how it feels, the situation is basically safe. Storytelling is not a dangerous occupation, and your work is valuable.

- You need not resist the feeling of fear. It may even belong in your performance.

Read on for the details!

EXCITEMENT AND FEAR

There are two basic causes of what we call "performance anxiety": excitement (or readiness) and fear. They share a similar physiology. I remember reading about early social psychology experiments (of dubious ethics from today's viewpoint) in which subjects were secretly injected with a form of adrenaline. Some were put in a room with something beautiful; the others witnessed a staged fight. All of them were aroused by the chemical stimulant. But those who were in the presence of beauty described their sensations as excitement, while those who were in the presence of hostility described their sensations as fear.

In other words, there are two components of anxiety. One is the excitation that produces the familiar symptoms of increased heart-rate, blood rushing to the head, perspiration, dry mouth, etc. The other component is our assessment of the situation—either "This is a good situation; I am excited," or "There is danger here; I am afraid."

For storytelling, excitement is necessary but fear is expendable. This chapter starts by describing excitement. Then it goes on to explain fear and how it can be diminished and even put to use.

Readiness

Our bodies are miraculous in their ability to adapt to a variety of extraordinary occasions. We have all heard tales of people performing amazing feats in emergencies, such as lifting an auto single-handedly off an injured child.

Even telling a story in one-to-one conversation may require some mobilization of our mental and physical resources, as we focus our imagination, voices, and bodies to reexperience and communicate the importance of our narrative. Certainly, a performance in front of a group will require arousal if we are to do it well. This necessarily involves the speeding up and intensification of bodily functions such as circulation and breathing.

Too much arousal is an impediment. So is too little.

I remember my first time telling a story live on the radio. I was so excited that I could scarcely slow down enough to communicate. I was so overenergized that I remained alert far into the night.

The next time I entered a radio studio was to prerecord a story for later broadcast. Remembering my earlier adventure, I made an effort to stay calm. To my surprise, the *recording* environment was quite different from the *broadcasting* environment. Now the emphasis was less on being present in the moment than on getting a good "take." In my calm state I was not able to sustain a focused performance in the face of the dreary retakes. My internal engine was running too slowly for the load placed on it.

To be "revved up" is actually a gift. It helps me be present, ready to respond to the demands of the moment. Too little arousal slows and limits my reactions—whereas too much separates or distracts me from the present.

READINESS SKILLS INCREASE OVER TIME

When I think back to my most nervous moments, they are all related to "firsts:" my first public performance for children, my first solo show, my first time with an audience over three hundred people, my first time at the National Storytelling Festival.

One element of the nervousness at a "first" is that I don't know exactly how much readiness to muster. But after a few times in any given situation, I usually become less uncertain. I learn to muster just enough energy, so that my preparation seems "smooth" to me.

In fact, I may not even be aware of how energized I am becoming. I learned of this "hidden arousal" one night when I showed up for a "routine" performance near my home. Of course, I had been aware for several days that a performance was coming, and I had unconsciously visualized my periods of activity and rest leading in an arc to the performance evening. But my overall attitude was "This is no big deal."

When I arrived at the site this particular evening, my employer said, "Oh, no! Didn't you get the message? We had to cancel!" I was mildly annoyed, but, since I hadn't bothered to get excited about the show (I thought), I was not especially upset about missing it. I just went home and settled in for a quiet evening.

Not quite! I soon discovered that I was completely "revved," and remained overenergized for hours. I finally went out for a run, and even then couldn't sleep until long past my bedtime.

Evidently, I had prepared myself for a precise expenditure of energy, at a particular point in the evening. When that energy was not called for after all, I was left overstimulated. Only then did I appreciate how finely tuned my system had become to the needs of my performances.

ONE UNCERTAINTY AT A TIME

Part of learning to be ready is learning to separate the factors that make for uncertainty. Then I can work on them one at a time.

If I'm planning to perform for a new kind of *audience*, then I can reduce the overall level of uncertainty by telling them familiar stories. Or, if the familiar stories won't do, I can set up in advance some relatively safe "practice audiences" for trying out the new stories.

If a *story* itself is new to me—or challenging for some other reason—I can find ways to practice it on less demanding audiences. My two-act story, "The Soul of Hope," for example, provided me with many challenges over its first thirteen years. At a certain point it became clear to me, first, that it was succeeding with small, congenial audiences, and, second, that I needed to tell it another twenty or thirty times just to hone the story. After those additional performances, I thought, I might be able to reach out to larger audiences or to people less attuned to the story—but it would be silly to take on more challenging audiences while the story itself remained such a challenge. For a time, then, I actively pursued paid "house concerts" and other venues that involved small, well-selected audiences.

The third variable, after the audience and the story, is *myself.* The longer it has been since I've told a particular story—or any story at all—the more anxious I become about performing. Every fall, my first school performance brings up a crisis in my self-confidence. If, as sometimes happens, I've gone a month or two without telling *any* stories, I face enormous doubts about my ability, my right to tell, and the value of my stories.

In other words, the voice of confidence weakens over time without being buttressed by positive experience, but the voice of doubt may remain strong. (The second half of this chapter contains tips for weakening it.) The longer it has been since my last success, the greater the relative strength of my uncertainty.

Please note that I have been telling professionally for many years, yet I still notice this effect—and I know other seasoned tellers who have had similar experiences. When I talk with beginning tellers who may go several months between tellings, and who have a much smaller store of positive experiences to draw on, I am humbled that they have the bravery to tell at all.

You can avoid this common form of performance anxiety simply by telling stories often. If fear prompts you to try compulsive rehearsing, try setting up a series of friendly audiences instead. Without making your telling inflexible and unresponsive to your audience (as fear-driven solo practicing might), successful performances will bolster your confidence.

Fear

If readiness is necessary and tends to help a storyteller, fear is unnecessary and tends to hinder. Fear can show up before I tell, as "performance anxiety" or reluctance to work on stories. It can numb me to the feelings in my story, making it feel "flat." It can also interfere with my relationship with my listeners. To reduce the harmful effects of fear on my storytelling, I need first to know what it is.

What Is Fear?

Fear seems to be a "lower-level" neurological function that mobilizes us to face danger. Like other emotions, it is essentially involuntary. As such it probably has served as a "backup system" to protect us.

Suppose, for example, that we are relaxedly absorbed in noticing the flowers beside the path while ignoring the leopard crouched ahead of us. In this dangerous situation, fear can grab us, focusing all our attention on the threat. Once we've become alerted to the leopard, we are not likely to be thinking about the flowers anymore—at least until we have removed ourselves from danger and returned to our normal mode of relaxed, intelligent interaction with our environment.

Unfortunately, fear doesn't go away as easily as it comes. While the transition to fear can be instantaneous, the transition from fear back to normal functioning requires some neurological processing. After we reach safety, we tremble, shake, sweat, and laugh about our close call. When this process is done, all information that came in during the fear episode will be available for recall, just like our observations about the flowers on the path. Further, we will be able to remember the leopard incident freely—or tell a story about it—without once again feeling afraid.

Fear can come back years later to haunt our storytelling because, if the transition process does not finish, it leaves some information still stored in the emotionally charged "fear mode." Then, any reminder of the fear episode can become a trigger for the transition process. A strong experience of safety—such as the relaxed embrace of a loved one or the smiles of a delighted audience—can trigger it, too.

Here's where it gets tricky. While we are processing fear, we may think we are in danger again. In this case, we mistake the reexperienced feeling for new information about the *present*, tempting us to enter "fear mode" in this new situation. This not only further postpones the transition back to normal thinking, it adds a new dose of "fear mode" information, which will require still more processing at a later time.

Thus, the experience of fear is of two kinds. One kind—extremely rare in a performance situation—is a potentially useful response to present danger. The more common kind is the re-experiencing of past, unprocessed fear, as our organism attempts to complete the needed transition process.

HOW TO PROCESS FEAR

If I process fear as it comes up, it has no lasting effect on me. But if I do not, it snowballs. Since our society tends to shun the processing of fear, people often end up with large amounts of fear that they learn to avoid, ignore, or act out.

As a storyteller, I am better off when I process my fear than when I live with it. I become more relaxed about performance. I am better able to imagine frightening scenes and heroic deeds. I become a more flexible judge of my listeners' responses and emotional needs.

I achieve these benefits by processing my old fear regularly. My personal way of doing this work is to schedule regular sessions with "feelings buddies." Most of these sessions occur far from my storytelling venues, but I will sometimes set one up just before a performance in whatever off-stage location is available. An impromptu session may last only five or ten minutes, but I devote forty to sixty minutes to my regular ones.

During these sessions, I try to find a way to enter the transition process for pent-up fear. I know I am succeeding when I laugh, tremble, shake, or sweat. Whenever I find a way to make one of these happen, I persist as long as it keeps working or until I run out of time.

How do I get myself laughing or trembling in the first place? To process fear, I need to notice that I am now *safe*. That is why I use a buddy when possible, for the safety of another human standing guard relaxedly while I do this inner work. Then I find a way to direct my attention that establishes my safety. If one attempt does not work, I keep trying others.

Sometimes it works just to notice my safe environment. "Okay," I might say, "There is no one here to hurt me or humiliate me. I am an adult, and you are here to protect me if I were to need it." Other times, I may need to refer indirectly to the terrors of my past, saying, "I survived!" or "I am safely out of his clutches!"

Often, focussing on a small piece of safety can have a bigger effect than trying to notice my overall freedom from danger. "Well, there is no one trying to kill me *at this moment*," I might try saying, or "It has been known to happen at least once in the history of the world that someone actually made it!" It might even work to focus on some ordinary detail of nature or a benign image from a story, thereby establishing indirectly that no crisis is actually threatening my life at the moment.

Here are some other statements that might help you notice a small but undeniable element of safety. You can make up your own:

- *Storytelling is not a lethal art. There have been no known performance fatalities.*
- *Somewhere in the world, right now, someone is speaking freely and easily, with a great sense of confidence.*
- *People have been known to be seen—and survive.*
- *Once upon a time, someone actually spoke in his or her true voice—and the world rejoiced.*

Or, you can approach an awareness of safety from unexpected directions:

- *Does anyone really think that a little stark terror will stop ME?*
- *Humiliation? I eat humiliation for breakfast!*
- *I may die, but I'm actually brave enough to tell a story to these unarmed people.*

Another paradoxical technique is to take on a role other than victim. For example, I can scorn my fear, saying something like, "Bring on the criticism! Is that the worst you can say about my story?" Or I can actively take the role of victimizer, saying with a tone of relish,

"I am not the one who is stupid. You are!" In all these cases, the exact truth of my statement is not the point, rather that I can use it to trigger the processing of my old fear.

Stories are often useful, too. In my story, "The Chicken Woman," an entire community is faced with death if no one steps forward to undergo a test. All refuse out of fear until a humble poultry dealer says, "I'll do it! Why not? We'll all die anyway!" When I say these words in a fear session, I begin to laugh.

Each of these techniques works best if I use several elements of oral language. An open stance, defiant gesture, or confident posture can be the key tool in establishing my safety and therefore in allowing me to process old fear.

NOTICING THE ACTUAL SITUATION

The long-term solution to performance fears is to process my old fear. But what do I do in the short term?

When I am not actually processing fear, I want to be present in the moment. I want to direct my attention back onto my current reality. Here are some techniques for reminding myself of the truth:

1. Welcoming my readiness. I can distinguish the symptoms of readiness from the emotional experience of fear.

2. Noticing the humanity of the audience. I can note individuals and try to connect with them through my eyes and facial expressions—even, in the right circumstances, by moving closer to them or addressing them individually. I can focus, at least some of the time, on the those who seem to be responding the most positively.

3. Noticing that I am not in danger. (If I am in danger, of course, I should deal with it!) I can notice that no one is aiming a gun at me, growling at me, or otherwise threatening my safety.

4. Noticing that I am valuable. I have gifts to give these people: the gift of the story, of the magic of storytelling, of imagination, of my own point of view. I can focus on my intention of offering something I love.

5. Noticing that I have allies. There may be people present whom I trust. There may be someone who invited me and hopes that I do well. (If I bomb, that person will likely be in deeper trouble than I.) At the very least, my listeners want me to do well. As Donald Davis

says, "No audience member goes to a performance saying, 'Boy, I hope this is dreadful.'"

6. Noticing that I am in a position of power. I have the floor. I may even be on a stage, physically above them. I may have amplification for my voice—they don't! I've had a chance to experience my story before; for them, it's all new and surprising. If I am improvising, I am the one in charge of what happens in my story and how long it lasts; they are at my mercy. Unless I am a child or a prisoner, I can leave at any time. (It may cost me something to walk out, but I'm not stuck there.) If I am a visiting storyteller, I never need to see these people again.

7. Noticing that the people I may feel afraid of are not really paying much attention to me. Even if my audience is sitting cross-armed and scowling, they are probably paying much more attention to themselves than to me. Look at them! They are miserable! What makes me think they notice me enough that their opinions could possibly matter?

Over time, I may find that individual techniques gain and lose effectiveness. It may help me during one period to focus on some aspect of myself, such as my power or goodness, my breath which carries my voice to my audience, or my feelings about the story. In another situation, it may help more to focus on the imagery or message of the story itself. In still another, it may work better to focus on my relationship with the audience (my love or respect for them, my empathy with their struggles) or even on the context of the storytelling event (how honored I am to tell in this place).

There is a problem with using these techniques. Their very effectiveness may tempt me to try substituting them for emotional processing. This will not work for long! The decision to postpone the processing of fear can be compared to the decision to postpone sleep when I am tired. I can do it at any one moment, but the longer I go without meeting my need for it, the less functional I become. If I keep working on my old fears, however, I will have an ever-increasing ability to keep my attention on the present—and to respond to it freely, creatively, and flexibly.

SPEAKING BACK TO COMMON WORRIES

For all your work processing old fears and noticing the current reality, you may sometimes get stuck trying to answer one of your own anxieties. Here are a few common worries, with some suggested points of view to take on each one:

1. What if I forget an important part of my story? This is not a major problem! Just memorize this partial sentence: "What you don't know about ____ is ____."

Let's say you are telling "Jack and the Beanstalk." Just at the point where the giant chases Jack out of the castle the first time, you realize that you completely forgot to tell about the beanstalk. You left out a major portion of the beginning of the story, including how Jack got to the giant's castle. And that means that Jack has no beanstalk to climb back down!

You always have the option, in a case like this, to complete the sentence you memorized. You can say something like, "What you don't know about Jack is that he was very poor. Way back before he ever heard of the giant, his mother gave him their only cow to sell, and Jack traded it for three beans. He planted the beans, and there grew an enormous beanstalk. He climbed it—and that's how he got to the giant's castle! So when the giant was chasing Jack, Jack just jumped onto the beanstalk and slid down it!"

2. What if I stammer or hesitate? Good news! These stones in the stream of talk usually convey an aura of sincerity. If someone pauses to search for words, we take it as a sign that the speaker is deeply involved in what he is saying. In fact, a too-slick delivery can convey insincerity.

3. What if I go completely blank? This happens to everyone some time or other. Pause. Breathe. If you can't even remember what you just said, you can always ask your audience for help: "Now, where was I?" Or let them give you some ideas to react to: "What do you suppose happened next?" In the worst case, you can leave the story and start another: "We're going to leave Jack there for a while. Now, a thousand years before Jack came along, there was a woman in Persia…" If you remember the rest of the story later, your audience may be even more grateful than usual to hear its ending.

4. What if I don't do well, and they never hire me again? Two choices: either this is an appropriate context for you, or it's not. If it's not, it is preferable that they *don't* hire you away from the contexts that let you shine. If this is an appropriate context, on the other hand, you now have a chance to notice what problems you need to solve. It's better to learn now in one big failure than to peter out slowly over many lackluster performances that would waste many opportunities and still never bring the problems into sharp focus.

5. What if I cry at the part that moves me? Great! You've just established your deep emotional connection to your story!

6. What if they think I'm crazy? This one deserves longer treatment than I can give it here. "Crazy" is a hurtful label often applied to people whose need to process painful emotion is much greater than what the society generally allows. By applying the most terrible sanctions to some people (taking them away from their homes and communities, locking them up, drugging them) the society scares most of the rest of us into "functioning" with less resource for emotional processing than we really need. In the face of such an implied threat, it makes sense that speaking emotionally and creatively would bring up your fear of being called "crazy." But look at it this way: you are proudly demonstrating what it is like to stand beyond the pale of "normal" behavior. You are a lead ewe who has crossed the harmless fence wire and is showing the other sheep that they need no longer be penned in!

You may find yourself focused on some other worry that is not on this list. In that case, you can apply some general principles to counter whatever concern has stolen your attention.

The first principle is that the real consequences of whatever you are worried about are probably much smaller that you think. After all, this is a symptom of fear needing to be processed, not of a real problem to be solved. (If it were mostly a real problem, you would be engaged in solving it, not experiencing fear about it.)

The second principle is that nothing has *only* negative consequences. Every problem represents a corresponding strength (just as every strength corresponds to a potential problem). You think you're too serious? You probably have a gift for seeing importance and meaning. You think you're an emotional lightweight? You probably have a gift for lightness and changing perspectives.

The third principle is that it's almost always possible to recover from a misstep. You got them to laugh at what should have been the saddest moment? Rest assured that there is some way to lead them into the deep feeling that lies under their laughter. You started telling a fifteen-minute mystical story that, after three minutes, turns out to be incomprehensible to your listeners? Change stories! You can just stop in the middle, saying something like, "Well, that's a story for another day. Did you know that there are dozens of stories about the Jack from 'Jack in the Beanstalk?' Here's one from the Kentucky mountains…"

Worries are usually 90 percent fear, 10 percent problem. There is no rationality to the *fear,* except its own logic as a burr in your emotional saddle that wants to be removed through the transition process. The *problem,* on the other hand, has a benign rationality that may be helpful to focus on: it has relatively small consequences, contains its own advantages, and can be solved.

WHEN FEAR CAN BE USEFUL

Focusing on my safety can be highly effective. But it may tempt me to move from *noticing* that I am not in danger (which is useful) to *pretending* that I don't feel afraid (which cuts me off from part of my emotional resources). Similarly, I grew up with the message, "Fear is to be resisted. Fight against it!" This idea, too, can corrupt my attempts to simply notice the present.

As a result, there are times when it helps me, even in performance, to allow the feeling of fear to run through me. Fear can be my ally when dealing with my feelings of vulnerability as I tell, with a character's feelings within a story, or with the issues a story raises for me.

First, being a storyteller involves being open to the audience. I reveal my thoughts, emotions, and enthusiasms, while my listeners have the privilege of concealing theirs. I need to keep myself open to their responses so that I can react appropriately. If I were to close off all feelings of vulnerability, the audience might unconsciously interpret me as being closed off to *them.* Therefore, I try to recognize, even welcome my fear of them—in the context of my knowledge that I am safe, valuable, and powerful. Allowing the spice of fear to flavor the stew of confidence can actually allow my performances a depth they would otherwise lack.

Second, my fear may help me portray a character. And the character's fear may help me with my own.

Jay O'Callahan sometimes feels fearful and closed before telling a story of his childhood, "Glasses." A key character in this story, Jay's Aunt Anne, is a Japanese-American who has been persecuted by her fellow Bostonians during World War II. Afraid to leave her house, she is enticed out on a hot summer day by young Jay, who wants her to share the fun of poking a "tar bubble" in the street. Getting her to leave the sanctuary of her home is the first "extraordinary" thing young Jay has done. The story ends after the war at the wedding of Jay's anti-Japanese war hero, Uncle Jackie. Perhaps emboldened by her foray onto the street with Jay, Aunt Anne comes to the reception. The uncle takes her hand and dances with her. And young Jay knows the war is finally over.

When Jay feels anxious before telling this story, he thinks of Aunt Anne's fear and withdrawal. He thinks, "Aunt Anne didn't want to open the door to the boy—but the boy kept inviting her." Rather than suppress his fear, Jay uses it as an entree into her character. In the process, Jay is reminded of the boy's fearlessness. Without denying his own feeling of fear, Jay finds it—and its antidote—within his story.

Third, a story's themes may trigger fear. If I find myself feeling afraid as I prepare to tell, I can ask myself, "Where does fear relate to what I most want to convey in this story?" Suppose that my answer, for a personal story, is "I want people to know what it was like growing up in my particular circumstances," I can then ask myself where fear fits into the answer. Was it sometimes frightening to be a child? Was it humiliating to talk about some or all of my experience? Were consequences threatened if I revealed "family secrets"?

In my Jewish mystical story, "The Soul of Hope," there are strong images of hopefulness. Thinking about my own feelings of fear and grief that have come up as I told the story, I realized that, like many children and young adults, I was frequently subject to hurt around my hopefulness. My expectations that everything could be improved and that everyone was worthy of concern were often greeted with accusations of naivety and ignorance. The fear of receiving more humiliation usually accompanies my telling of the story—and this fear is relevant to the subject matter. In fact, my emotional presence has been increased by my willingness to feel fear as I tell the story, in order to be fully hopeful.

17

Your Support Team

For many of us, creating a support team is the key way to grow. As storytellers, we do many invisible and unpaid tasks, such as experimenting with oral language, finding structure in stories, setting up supportive audiences for practicing, and warming up our voices. If we do these things, they will help us solve important problems. But how do we get them done?

You may be one of the rare people who does all your significant tasks without help. But for most of us, a helper can make the difference between getting certain jobs done and just wanting to. Knowing how to create and maintain your support team, therefore, is essential to improving your storytelling.

Planning Buddies

For over a decade I thought about a particular project, saying to myself, "I want to get to that some day"—but, of course, I never seemed to. Many projects that were only for my artistic development seemed to be usurped again and again by trivial, daily tasks and by projects that I was paid for or that I was doing for the sake of others. My personal priorities seemed to come last.

Once, while leading a coaching workshop, I heard myself saying to another storyteller, "If you find yourself not getting to something, you must need help with it." Eventually, I decided to take my own advice. I would get help with making sure that I spent time on what mattered the most to me.

As a result, I recruited a "planning buddy" who was to help me keep my personal, long-term needs on the front burner. I made a regular monthly appointment to check in on the big issues in my storytelling. I figured that if I had someone to report to once a month, I would at least be reminded of what I had meant to do but not done, before too long a period had gone by.

Later, I added other planning buddies for particular projects. In all cases, their role was straightforward. Their first task was to listen to my successes from the previous month. Second, I wanted them to make sure that I did not forget anything important to me that was still undone. Finally, they were to push me to decide exactly what I wanted to do about what remained.

I realized at some point that I could meet with planning buddies over the telephone rather than in person. This allowed me to call on potential buddies who lived far away.

Many Helpings

A few years ago, I confided to a friend that I was having trouble keeping my office neat. She said, "Why don't you get someone to help you go through the piles of papers?" I stared at her. What? I thought that putting things away was something you just had to do yourself.

Over the years, I have expanded my list of things that it is possible to get help with. At any one time, I may not need helpers for all of them. But just realizing that I can get help has been liberating.

Most commonly, I use rehearsal buddies (peer coaches) to listen to me while I "talk through" new stories, tell stories, or think aloud about issues in stories. I also use these sessions to plan upcoming performances and workshops.

I use other helpers to work on my core skills as a storyteller. I use "feelings buddies" and take classes to encourage the processing of emotional hurts. I have traded time with a voice teacher in exchange for coaching. I have hired people to work with me on my physical movements in performance.

Some support team members help me manage the daily business of my storytelling life. This includes those who listen to me while I decide what to write in brochures, proposals, and grant applications. I write my books and articles in the presence of "writing buddies." And I hire or barter with people who put labels on envelopes, maintain my mailing list, and answer my phone a few hours a week.

Finally, I have helpers who assist me with the larger issues. Such buddies help me keep my larger career goals in mind, help with specific projects, and even help me manage the rest of my support team.

Three Kinds of Helpers

I use three basic kinds of helpers: hired help, "parallel play-mates" and "barter buddies." Hired helpers work by the hour for money, giving me clerical help or professional assistance.

Parallel playmates work on their own tasks while I work on mine, re-creating the idea of "library dates" or "study halls." For example, I have a writing buddy. We get together every week to work on our individual writing. We begin and end each session with ten minutes of checking in with each other. In the middle, we write separately, but we know we can ask for five minutes of being listened to, if one of us gets stuck or overwhelmed.

Parallel playmates don't have to be doing the same task. Some don't even see each other. They check in via phone. Just knowing that someone is aware of what they are doing is all they need.

"Barter buddies," unlike parallel playmates, divide their time together. Each acts as helper for half the time and gets helped for the remainder.

Some barter buddies offer each other different services. For example, I coached one storyteller who then consulted with me for an equal amount of time about marketing. Another helper bartered one hour of my consulting time (in which I helped her with her storytelling business) for four hours of her time filing papers for me.

Some barter buddies trade time at each session. But you can also "keep an open account," taking or giving help as needed even if it takes a while to balance out.

The Care and Feeding of Helpers

To find a voice teacher or a computer instructor, I need to start searching among those who have the skills. In such a case, I usually begin by asking around for recommendations. But many of my helping roles require only that the person be able to listen to me well—or do mundane tasks without making me feel stupid for needing help. When I'm looking for the latter kind of helper, I start by asking myself, "Who would I like to spend more time with?"

Once I have a list of possible helpers, I call one up and set up a one-time appointment. If it works well, we can schedule more. If not, I have lost little and can try another from the list.

Having found a helper I want to continue with, my work is still not done. My helping relationships need careful thought and periodic review.

I find that it's important for me to give my helpers clear instructions. Much unsuccessful help can be traced to miscommunication, as when I'm hoping for someone to listen while I think, whereas my helper thinks I want his opinion.

Some helpers require a lot of training before they can give me the kind of help I want, especially when I need someone to change modes several times in the course of a session. But almost anyone can learn to be supportive, if I'm clear, persistent, and calm.

Naturally, some helpers just seem to "click" with me, intuiting when to intervene and when to just "beam attention" at me. Like good friends, good helpers are among life's treasures. Like good friendships, good helping relationships are worth constructing and maintaining.

Intangible Help

I set up helping relationships in order to solve particular problems. Perhaps I need someone to keep me company while I pay my bills or to pay attention to me while I make phone calls that feel difficult. But the benefits often exceed my concrete goals.

Storytellers, like all artists, face popular misconceptions about our work. Instead of being viewed as a means to understand our true nature, our art is seen as a frill. Instead of being honored as conveners of community, storytellers are often relegated to the oddball fringe. Furthermore, all artists struggle against the idea that unless you are famous you are not any good, and against the notion that "talent" belongs only to the few.

My weekly visits with members of my support team put me in contact with people who remember the importance of my work and my abilities. When I start to succumb to the messages that sap my confidence, my helpers are there to remind me what I can do and why it's important.

Further, our society—with its emphasis on the individual—tends to make us view ourselves in isolation. Living in contact with a support team helps me remember that I need, thrive in, and can have a web of connection to others.

Like all other important and difficult tasks, storytelling will succeed better if I have allies and friends. (See the Appendix: How to Find Storytelling Organizations and Publications for ways to contact organizations that can enlarge your circle of colleagues still further.) Without allies, I can only take on what one person alone can do. With them, I can be more effective and have more fun.

Putting It All Together

The premise of this book is that you, the storyteller, will tell a story best when you continue to shape it and to respond to your listeners as you tell. You will create a dynamic balance—taking into account the nature of the transfer of imagery—among the demands of the storyteller, the listeners, and the story.

Each component of the storytelling event has been explored in previous chapters. In the end, however, the components are only important insofar as they contribute to the overall effect of the storytelling event—an indivisible whole.

How do you combine the parts to make the whole work? That is the subject of this final section.

Chapter 18 introduces an amazing tool—namely, your attention: what you think about as you tell. Your attention shifts spontaneously from one component to another. It usually moves just where it is needed to help integrate the complex mechanics of your storytelling. Fortunately, there are ways to free your attention when it is blocked from moving flexibly.

Chapter 19 shows how you can direct your attention in a way that helps connect each moment in a story to your overall goals for the storytelling event. In some cases this connection will require discovering only a single concept; in others, it will require drawing on all your knowledge of the storytelling triangle.

Finally, the Conclusion takes up the mystery of transformation—the sometimes elusive result of perfect balance among all the components of the storytelling event.

18

THE FLEXIBLE SHIFTING OF ATTENTION

When you tell a story, you do many things at once. You use all the elements of oral language: you speak, gesture, and change your posture. You imagine the story. You respond to the audience. You have your own feelings, both about the story and about the event. You might also be thinking about what's coming next in your story, about what just happened in your story, and about any number of other things. With all these activities happening at once, what are you actually thinking about? Where is your attention as you tell?

Your attention—what you think about—is, oddly, seldom thought about. Nonetheless, it is a powerful tool for integrating the components of the storytelling event. In this chapter, you'll learn about the four layers of your attention that relate directly to the mechanics of storytelling. You'll learn how your attention shifts naturally among those four layers. You'll learn about obstacles that prevent this easy flexibility and some ways to overcome them.

Four Layers of Attention

My attention is usually divided among at least four areas. Three are components of the storytelling event, while the fourth is my judgment about what to do with the rest of what I notice.

When I tell a story, some of my attention is always on the *story*—imagining its events, emotions, meanings, and progression. Typically, the story absorbs the largest portion of my attention.

Some of my attention is always on the *audience* and my relationship to them. How are they doing? What do they need now?

Another portion of my attention is focused on *myself,* noticing my own physical and emotional state.

A final portion of my attention is reserved for what I call my *judgment:* the part of me that balances the needs of the first three parts and makes decisions about what to do. Should I sing the song an extra time here? What story should I tell next? Am I so angry at the child who keeps interrupting that I need to attend to my anger before I explode? Should I find a place later to insert the line I just omitted, or should I leave it out altogether? Should I stop and have them close the window or should I continue in the cold?

My "judgment" may also deal with the transfer of imagery and the context in which I am telling. My audience didn't seem to understand that last character's change of heart, perhaps because they can't see my facial expression. Should I try to use gestures more, instead? Why are they laughing in this part of the country whenever I pronounce a particular word? Should I take longer to imagine here, or speed up to let the audience imagine at a faster pace?

These four portions of my attention are diagrammed in figure 11. The left-hand portion ("Case 1") shows the proportions of my attention in a "typical" performance situation.

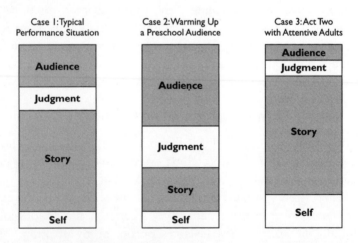

Figure 11: Where Is My Attention As I Tell a Story?

WARMING UP A PRESCHOOL AUDIENCE

In each situation, my attention will be distributed among the four areas—the story, my listeners, my self, and my judgment—in a unique proportion. To see the variation in how much of my attention is devoted to each of these four areas, imagine an extreme example: beginning a performance for a preschool audience ("Case 2" in the diagram).

In this case, my attention is mostly on my audience, the children. I have to establish my relationship with them, help them focus on me rather than on each other or the environment, and communicate my expectations both of how much fun this can be and of what they must do and not do during the performance.

At this beginning part of a preschool performance, a substantial portion of my attention is also on my judgment. Should I act sillier to engage them, or appear more sober to prevent them from getting too wild? Should I say something to the adult in the back who is letting the toddler walk through the seated youngsters? Will they be able to handle the quiet story I had planned to do next, or do they need something that will let them participate almost continuously?

A smaller portion of my attention is devoted to the story I am telling. Of course, I need to be imagining the story fully enough that I can actually tell it, but I don't have a lot of attention to spare. As a result, I prefer to begin a preschool program with a story that I know very well—and that therefore requires a minimum of my attention. New stories or difficult stories may require more attention in this situation than I have available.

At this point in my performance for preschoolers, only the bare minimum of my attention is reserved for myself. I might notice if I hurt myself or heard my pants rip, but I will probably not register small shifts in my emotional fine tuning or that my leg muscles are slightly more tense than I would like.

ACT TWO WITH ATTENTIVE ADULTS

For a contrasting example, consider the second half of a full-evening performance with an appreciative adult audience ("Case 3" in the diagram). The audience has long since accepted my invitation, and has settled down for a deep exploration of a leaning-back story.

At this point, little of my attention is devoted to my audience. I pay just enough attention to them that I will notice if something goes wrong, just as a parent might glance every once in a while at a deeply sleeping child.

Neither do I devote much of my attention to my judgment. Things are under control, and there are almost no major decisions to be made.

The bulk of my attention in this situation is reserved for the story itself. I can imagine it deeply, on many levels. I can hold in my mind several layers of its complexity. In fact, the more deeply and completely I imagine the story in this circumstance, the more the audience can enjoy it.

Since I can devote so much attention to the story, I can succeed with one that is perhaps less familiar. As long as I can keep my mistakes or uncertainties from interfering with the audience's deep immersion in the tale, I can afford to take a chance with a new (or older and partly forgotten) story.

Finally, I can devote more than the minimum of attention to myself. With a story that is not challenging for me, I may need very little attention for myself. But if the story challenges me physically, cognitively, or emotionally, in this situation I can afford to pay substantial attention to myself as I tell.

In my show "The Soul of Hope," for example, I still find that experiencing each emotional moment of the story demands a great deal of my attention. Thus, I need to check in with myself frequently during the tiny pauses: "Okay, Doug, take a breath. Empty yourself of the feeling from the last scene...Here comes the painful moment when his friend dies; be vulnerable to the terrible shock of it...Now, don't go on until you are fully there in his grief..."

Keeping My Attention Flexible

As the previous pages describe, when I tell a story my attention is divided among myself, the audience, the story, and my judgment. The relative proportions vary according to the circumstances.

How do I know my attention is where it belongs? Fortunately, the apportioning of my attention does not usually require my direct intervention.

When things are working well, in fact, my attention shifts freely and effectively to where it is needed. One day, for example, I was telling a Japanese version of "Tom Thumb" to a large group of second- and third-graders in a gymnasium. At one point, the tiny hero grabs a pigeon feather (which is taller than he is), dips it in ink, and "writes his parents a little note." Although I tell much of this story sitting down, I act out his writing of the "little note" by striding quickly back and forth across the floor as though the floor is a scrap of paper and I am a one-inch-tall writer. The physical reminder of the amount of effort required by a one-inch person to cross a six-inch piece of paper is humorous; as usual, this group of students laughed. My attention at this point in the story was divided approximately as shown in the left-hand side of figure 11 (Case 1: typical performance situation).

As it happened, however, I tripped and fell onto one knee just as I completed the movement sequence. Suddenly, my attention shifted its proportions. For the moment, the story left my attention almost completely. Much of my attention was on my knee, which hurt! As I stood up, I paid some attention to the audience. Had they noticed that I hurt myself? Were they worried about me? As I simultaneously took in information about the injury to my knee and the still-happy faces of the audience (they seemed to think it was all part of my performance), I momentarily devoted the largest part of my attention to judging what to do. Did my knee require immediate care? Was I able to continue? Did the audience need me to reassure them? If this clumsy fall was taken to be part of the story, was the story materially changed?

Making a quick judgment, I decided that I was able to continue, that the audience was fine, and that the story was not harmed. Turning my attention back to the story, I continued my tale. Naturally, I kept a little extra attention on my knee and my judgment, in case my assessment had to be changed. Otherwise, my attention remained primarily on the story and secondarily on the audience, just as it had been directed before I fell.

All this shifting of multiple portions of my attention happened without effort on my part.

OBSTRUCTIONS THAT MISDIRECT MY ATTENTION

In general, I can let my attention range freely among the components of the storytelling event. Sometimes, however, I need to pay attention to my attention. One such time is when an obstruction misdirects it.

When I feel that the person who has arranged for me to tell stories is treating me disrespectfully, for example, I may feel distractingly angry. In this case, my emotional response keeps my attention on the disrespect when it would probably be better applied to the current situation with my audience. In order to redirect my attention, I ask myself, "What is the gift I want to offer this particular audience?" Once I answer that question, I purposely keep my attention on the answer. In short, I direct my attention to my desired intention toward the audience.

In the case of the "Soul of Hope" (discussed in chapter 11, The Four Tasks), I discovered that I carry an unconscious intention toward the audience that is based on unhealed emotional hurt: the hope that the audience will acknowledge my past great efforts. This hurt forms an obstruction in my relationship with the audience that diverts my attention from where it will help in the present. (Note that this diversion of my attention would not necessarily be unproductive if I were telling in the role of beneficiary. In that case, focusing on my desire for acknowledgment might enable me to heal some of this hurt.) To correct this misdirection of my attention, I think to myself, "I will show how much I love this story, and allow my listeners to decide about it for themselves."

Here's another example. I tell a story in which one particular humorous line depends on a character making a sudden transition from one attitude to another. First, he is complimenting someone; suddenly he expresses suspicion of the same person. When I perform this correctly, the audience will almost always laugh.

Here's the problem. Although another storyteller might not care whether the audience laughs, I look forward to their laughter. When I keep their upcoming laughter in mind as I perform the transition, however, I tend to move my focus toward the audience as I speak. This makes the character seem suspicious, not of the person he is talking to, but of the audience. As a result, the transition becomes unclear and is no longer funny. Therefore, I make a conscious effort while performing this line to keep my attention on the two attitudes of the character, not on the audience's response.

Please note that it seldom works to say to myself, "Don't think of how funny this is." An intention *not* to think of something is rarely effective. If an obstruction of some kind is causing me to misdirect my attention, then I need to find a positive, more productive direction for my attention.

MEETING MY OWN NEEDS—FOR THE GOOD OF OTHERS

Any unmet need of mine will tend to distract my attention from where it is most useful. Trying to tell a story while thirsty, for example, will make it at least a little more difficult to focus on the story, the audience, and my judgment about what needs doing at the moment. Therefore, it is a favor to my audience to take a drink of water so that I am not distracted by a real, meetable, current need.

To be sure, I must always make a decision whether a particular need is worth meeting. If I begin to tell a story and realize that I forgot to make a promised phone call, for instance, I have to judge whether it makes more sense to interrupt the story to make the call or to continue the story while trying not to worry.

It is not possible to *meet* past needs—like my previously mentioned desire to have the audience acknowledge my lifetime of effort; this is actually based on an old hurt, which can only be healed. But many realistic current needs are worth meeting. If I need ginger tea or hot lemon-water to keep my vocal apparatus warm and clear, it is probably worth carrying an insulated bottle or making sure that someone provides it for me. If I tell better with certain arrangements of the physical space or after fifteen minutes alone for warm-up, it is a favor to my audience to make sure those needs are met.

Even less "ordinary" needs may be well worth meeting, if they free my attention. In the "Soul of Hope" performances, I realized at one point that I could not maintain my determination to offer the story no matter how the audience responded—unless I could tell that at least one person was enjoying the performance. Therefore, I made sure that at each performance at least one friend of mine was in the audience—chosen from among those whom I knew loved the story and could show their love of it on their faces as they listened. I also arranged with a "feelings buddy" to spend five minutes listening to me before each act, so that I could renew my intention in the presence of an understanding friend.

Whatever actual needs I have, finding a creative way to meet them may free my attention. This, in turn, allows me to direct my attention to the part of the storytelling event that most matters. In other words, I am free to use my attention to meet the needs of my listeners.

19

BALANCING THE DETAILS WITH THE GOALS

I tell stories because I want them to affect my audience. But I can not accomplish anything by standing there and willing the audience to be affected. I have to do something concrete: speak words, make movements, change my facial expression. In order to achieve my goals, I need to get involved in the details of storytelling—from oral language and imagery, to the meaning and structure of a story, to my exact relationship to my listeners.

It can be difficult to keep both my goals and my concrete actions in mind at the same time. Storytellers, like most people, tend to focus on one domain or the other, the abstract or the concrete. Even books about storytelling usually focus either on the high mission and power of storytelling, on the one hand, or on the details of what to do and how to do it, on the other. The uniting of these two realms remains an unnamed, often unsolved problem.

How can I unite them? Going from the broad to the narrow, how can I get from a goal of an overall affect on the audience to a decision about how to tell a particular scene? Conversely, how can I immerse myself in the details of a particular scene without losing sight of my purpose in telling a story in the first place?

This chapter highlights two strategies. The first is to put the bulk of my attention on a single concept, such as the most important component of the storytelling event. The second, a refinement often needed for the most demanding parts of a tale, is to use a set of intermediate concepts that will help me experience how a moment in my story connects in several ways to my larger goals.

What Matters Most in This Event?

Often enough, I can use a single idea to tell each moment of a story in a way that supports my goals for the storytelling event. In previous chapters, I mentioned some such ideas that I have successfully focused on in the past:

- Think in the present.

- Keep the "Most Important Thing" about the story in my mind at all times.

- Be present emotionally.

- Show how much I love the story.

- Offer my story as a gift to the audience.

These ideas worked by putting my attention in a direction that happened to free me to be present and flexible. Others have *not* worked for me, such as "do my best," or "get it right." These ideas directed my attention where it becomes *in*flexible. When they were foremost in my mind, I used too much effort or else let my fears about mistakes distract me. Of course, you will have to find which ideas work or don't work for you.

Another useful focus is the most important component of a storytelling event. Just as there is a Most Important Thing for me in each story, so there may be a component of a storytelling event that matters most in a given situation. It may be the story, the listeners, or the storyteller. Or it may be a relationship between some of the other components.

For example, imagine that I am telling stories to an eight-year-old at bedtime. My head-cold (and resulting hoarseness) may not matter much; my forgetting parts of the story may not matter much; but if I am emotionally distant from my listener, the event may come to a grinding halt. In other words, the most important component of this event is probably my emotional closeness to my listener. If that is unobstructed, we may be transformed in spite of other obstructions.

It makes sense for me to try noticing the most important component in each situation. If I can't do everything perfectly, at least I can apply my efforts to what matters most.

Sometimes, as in the example of the bedtime story, the most important component is in my closeness to my listeners. In other cases, the key aspect may be in another facet of my relationship to them, such as their participation or my treating them respectfully.

Other times, however, the most important component may be in my relationship to the story: some part of its meaning, oral language, or imagery. I think of certain adult performances when my primary goal is to share the glory of beautiful language, or offer the healing power of a particular image, or help the audience enter into a particular culture's world-view. In these situations, of course, closeness to my listeners may still be important. It will make things go better. But if the key component is something about the story, my failure to be fully close with my listeners may not be crucial. It may not prevent achieving my goal.

Still other times, as when an audience is delighted to see me being myself in some way, or when I am the beneficiary of the storytelling event, the most important component may actually be my relationship to myself.

The most important component can even relate to the transfer of imagery itself. This might be true in a workshop on creativity (where imagining might be the aspect that matters most) or in a language class (where the use of oral language might be the aspect that matters most).

LEARNING THE MOST IMPORTANT COMPONENT

I may be aware of the most important component before the storytelling event. Other times, I can only recognize it as the event unfolds.

Several years ago, I flew to another state for two school assemblies. In the second performance (for ages 5–8), I told a story in which a monster tries to intimidate an old woman; she is terrified but stands up to the monster anyway. Until the point in the story when the old woman reacted to the monster, my audience was responding with substantial interest, as most such groups had always responded. At this point, however, their response became electrifying. They laughed uproariously at her defiant but terrified speech to the monster, with a kind of laughter that suggested a release of pent-up emotion. Naturally, I began to emphasize this aspect of the story, even though I was amazed by the strength of my audience's response.

As I continued my performance, still wondering what nerve the story had hit, I had a realization: as of that day, the United States and its allies were prepared at any moment to launch a military attack on Iraq. The children had been reacting to the imminence of war and the uncertainty of when it would begin. The image from my story of the old woman's fear and defiance was just what they required in order to release some of their emotional tension.

On that day, with that group, the most important component was a single piece of imagery from the story. I had not anticipated that it would be so central, but it became a point of connection between the components of the storytelling triangle. All I needed to succeed was enough clarity in my relationships to them, myself, and the story to enable me to convey this one image. Would any obstructions have mattered? No—so long as they let this key image come across.

INTERMEDIATE CONCEPTS

Thinking about the most important component of a storytelling event as I tell—or about some other single idea—can often be enough to help me connect details of the moment with my goals for the event. Sometimes, though, a single idea will not be an adequate focus. In such a case, I can try to understand more explicitly how each concrete decision and action is derived from my broadest goals.

Chapter 9: Memorizing deals with a somewhat similar problem: how to relate your purpose in telling a story to each word of it. The process suggested there involves creating a series of intermediate concepts—asking which sections, scenes, moments, and sentences link individual words to the overall meaning of the story.

Similarly, we can create a series of intermediate concepts that relate each detail of telling a story to our overall goal of transformation.

What are the intermediate concepts? They correspond roughly to the sections and chapters of this book.

My main areas of concentration, with their sub-areas, are:

I.   The transfer of imagery
     Sub-areas: a) oral language; b) the nature of imagery
II. The story
     Sub-areas: a) the meanings; b) the structure
III. The listeners
     Sub-areas: a) are they my helpers or the beneficiary? b) the stages of our process: uniting, inviting, offering, acknowledging; c) the kind of response I am producing (e.g., leaning forward versus back); d) where we are within a program of stories.
IV. My self
     Sub-areas: my body; my voice; my emotions; my helpers.

Each sub-area, of course, can be divided still further; the process of subdivision continues until the most concrete level is reached that is necessary to support a particular contribution to the overall achievement of the desired effect.

Connecting to the Moment

To understand the chain of connection that reaches from the goal for a storytelling event to the concrete actions of telling a story, consider an example.

In my story, "The Soul of Hope," there is a moment when the main character finds his best friend's dead body. In shock, he begins to cry. This moment, not too surprisingly, is difficult for me emotionally. I never want to feel his grief, to be sure—but what is hardest for me is his shock. Unconsciously, I try to protect myself from this unpleasant feeling of shock by "going numb" emotionally just before this moment.

In time, I will probably discover some of the unhealed emotional hurts behind my avoidance. When I have healed more of that hurt, his shock will no longer be as strongly charged for me, and I will be more willing to imagine it. Of course, this future healing, however useful, may not solve the problem completely, since the nature of shock may continue to make it difficult not to anticipate, no matter how much emotional processing I do.

Be this as it may, I still have my problem in the short term. How can I keep myself open to experiencing the main character's terrible feeling of shock at finding that his friend has died?

The solution has parts that correspond to the components of the storytelling event. I will find pathways of connection from this moment to my larger goal, one pathway leading through each component. These pathways (shown in figure 12) will focus my attention while I tell the story.

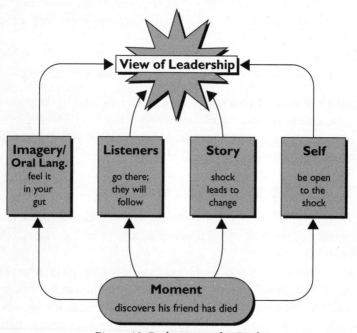

Figure 12: Pathways to the Goal

First, I will look at my goals. What kind of effect do I seek with this story? What do I want to have happen as a result of telling it?

With any story—especially a long, complex one like "The Soul of Hope"—there are many aspects to my goals. Yet it usually helps me to choose what I perceive to be the main goal, even if it changes in a few weeks or months.

So, forced to choose a key goal, I say, "The audience will have a new understanding about leadership—about changing the world."

At this point, I have four questions to ask myself. How does this moment of discovering his friend's death contribute to my goal—through each component?

Let's look at the story component first. From the point of view of leadership, the plot can be described as being about a character who will eventually take on the goal of changing the world. In particular, in this incident the main character learns that the mystical experiments he and his friend have attempted can have fatal results. His response to this tragedy, in turn, leads him to understand that he cannot continue to pursue his quiet, withdrawn life of mystical contemplation. He comes to see the death of his friend as part of a larger pattern of suffering which he then devotes his life to changing.

This means that, if he is not shocked by his friend's death, the change in his life's direction might not be plausible. Therefore, I have a new reason to feel his shock: it is important for a turning point in the plot which moves the character closer to certain actions—which, in turn, are essential for my goal of the audience's new understanding.

Here are my answers for the other three components:

1. In terms of imagery and oral language, I will feel this moment in my gut. I will use the kinesthetic imagery of the terrible feeling he feels in his gut as a metaphor for the aspect of the world that needs to be changed.

2. In terms of my relationship to my listeners, I have already mentioned a problem I have with this story: I tend to want to wait for their approval—but they are busy dealing with the complexity and depth of the story. Therefore, I have decided to take an attitude of just showing them how much I love the story. In this case, that attitude translates into a pledge to go deep into the feelings of the character without waiting for the audience's encouragement. If I want my listeners to gain a new understanding of leadership, I need to present the scene confidently enough for them to experience the imagery in it. In other words, "Go into the feelings, and the audience will follow me."

3. In terms of my self, I have already established that it won't help

me to "go numb" or otherwise distract myself just before this scene. Phrasing this positively, I decide to remain open to the shock. If I do, I will be a clear conduit for the essential emotion in this important scene.

WHICH ANSWER DO I KEEP CLOSEST?

So far, I found four connections between this moment in the story and my goal of listener transformation. Each connection revealed a particular aspect of the importance of this scene. Before I had asked myself the four questions, I just knew that this scene was uncomfortable but felt important. Now I know that in this scene the plot turns and the dangers emerge; further, I will handle it by being open to feeling the shock in my gut without waiting for my audience's approval.

All this *might* be enough to help me stay present in this moment of the story. (Indeed, in simpler stories, I may have only a single focus for the entire story.) In the case of the moment in "The Soul of Hope" when the main character's friend dies, it is not. To be sure, when I realize that this terrible moment is coming, I can imagine all four of the pathways that lead from it to my overall goal (that my audience will gain a new understanding of leadership). But in the exact moment when the character sees his friend's body, four pieces of knowledge are too many.

This is like sledding down an icy hill past a dangerous tree: when I'm approaching the tree from a distance, it helps to remind myself of a handful of things about steering, using my weight, aiming for the meadow at the bottom of the hill, etc. But when I'm at the crucial point just before the tree, all I can remember is one thing, such as: "Pass it on the left!"

In my story, which is the one thing to focus on?

Only trial and error can tell. I try focusing on first one then another of the pathways, until I find the one that works the best.

At this point, I have tried several possibilities in performance. The one that works best for now is to focus primarily on the pathway that leads through imagery: I have to feel his shock in my gut.

Interestingly, however, this focus by itself is not enough. I need another focus until right before the actual moment. In the sled example, it won't do to think, "Left! Left! Left!" all the way down the hill. Instead, I might think of maintaining my weight and aiming for the meadow until the exact moment of "Now, left!"

In the story, if I think "Gut!" too soon, I lose my sense of *what* I am to feel in my gut. Approaching the moment, I need to keep all the components in mind. But it seems to work best if, as I near the moment that I dread, I keep the story component in the foreground of my attention. I aim my attention in the general direction of the goal about leadership, keeping the story in the front of my mind, with my self and my attitude toward my listeners close behind. The use of kinesthetic imagery, the fourth component, seems almost as distant, at this point, as the overall goal, but it remains in my awareness. The relative "closeness" of the components is shown in figure 13.

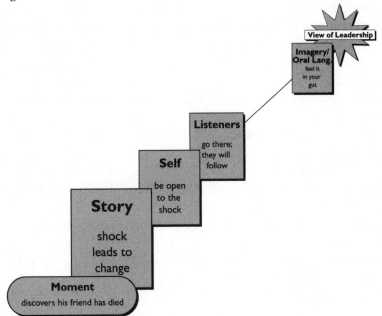

Figure 13: Components in the Foreground

When I focus on the story component of the scene (and switch at the last second to focusing on the imagery component), I am able to remain in the moment in a way that supports the most important aspect of the performance and therefore helps lead to transformation.

Creating the Strands of Connection

At last, we have answered the question, "How do I focus on my large goals and also on the details of what I am doing at the moment?" The answer is to create an understanding and awareness of how those details relate to your larger goals—and to keep a dynamic flexibility in shifting the focus.

The understanding and awareness comes from preparation, in which you explore various aspects of telling the story. The flexibility comes from a "game plan" that allows your attention to change its focus continually. If the story allows it, of course, your attention may remain on a single focus throughout. But if the story or the event demands it, you change your focus as you tell. You focus your attention at each moment on the aspect of your story that will move you closer to what matters most in a given storytelling event.

Whether you improvise stories completely or tell them word for word as someone else created them, you are an improvisational artist. You improvise with your attention. You turn it flexibly to first one then another of the strands that connect you with the story, with your listeners, with your self, and with your goals for the storytelling event.

No book like this one can explain *all* the strands of connection between your largest goal and all the details of your storytelling. But now that you know that it is important to your storytelling to understand these connections—and now that you understand several of them, you can continue your own explorations. On every level, your awareness of the components of the storytelling event helps you respond successfully to each unique moment of your storytelling adventures.

Conclusion: Transformation

Storytelling, this book maintains, takes place in the moment of interaction between you the storyteller and your listeners. As a practitioner of the imprecise art of transferring images, you must keep thinking in the present.

Your flexible awareness of the present will be informed by your knowledge of oral language and the nature of imagery. It will be supported by your deepening relationships to the story, your listeners, and yourself.

You will bring all this knowledge and experience to the present moment in a way that promotes your goals. At each moment, your attention will range flexibly over the mechanics of presenting the story as well as ways to connect the mechanics with your objectives. Your goals and your methods will be personal and appropriate to the entire constellation of each unique telling.

But even though you may enter each storytelling event with different goals, your successes will have something universal about them. Every highly successful storytelling event, like any successful artistic performance, *changes* the listeners and the storyteller. It changes them each internally, it changes their relationship, and it changes their relationships to the story. In short, it causes transformation.

Some tellers aim for lofty forms of transformation, such as wanting their listeners to experience a major shift in their sensibilities, be reminded of some aspect of who they really are, or form a connection with a body of traditional lore. Others seek shorter-term changes, such as understanding a single idea or having a few moments free from the demands of daily life. Large or small, these goals all involve change. If audience members seeking "entertainment" never change—never lose their preoccupation with the rest of their lives—then success has not happened.

This transformation within the listeners (and the storyteller) can happen without anyone having a precise sense of what just happened. People may seem more alert, "present," thoughtful, or energized than before the storytelling began. They may have a sense of an expanded awareness. They may feel more connected to the others present, or to the story. They may experience their transformation as a leap in understanding, as a miracle, as an experience of "flow," as a sense of being "right with the world," or merely as an unnoticed window through which they have viewed some large or small piece of life. Yet some kind of transformation happens in every case.

Transformation is intangible, yet it can be felt. I believe it occurs whenever the components of a storytelling event are integrated in just the right balance for that place, time, and group of people.

Transformation cannot be forced. But like the gardener preparing the ground, planting the seed, and tending the plants, you can take steps to make transformation possible. You can tell the story, asking questions about its structure, meaning, and images. You can develop your relationship to your listeners. You can work on your own needs, whether physical, mental, or emotional. You can work to understand how a story is imagined, communicated, and received. And then you must wait.

Transformation cannot be controlled or predicted. When it happens, it may be pleasant. It may even be ecstatic or awe-inspiring. It may also be terrifying. When the unity of the world clicks into focus, you may be put off balance by noticing your connection to something larger than yourself. Being big may mean giving up the reassuring boundaries of your smallness.

When transformation happens, you may not even notice it. In the grand, swirling flow of the river, you may lose sight of yourself, the individual swimmer. Since you will be changed by it, you cannot even guarantee that you—as you usually understand yourself—will be there as it happens.

This is an ultimate paradox of creativity and art: you work to make the miracle happen, but cannot determine if it will happen, when it will happen, or what form it will take. The parent must meet the predictable needs of the child while letting the child become an unpredictable individual. The farmer must prepare for the expected harvest, then let each plant in the orchard grow at its own pace, with its own number of fruit.

As a teller of stories, you develop your understanding and your experience with each component of the storytelling event. You prepare the way for transformation, then humbly allow it to sweep you up—or leave you on the shore continuing to build your skiff in anticipation of the next uncontrollable high water.

It is the nature of storytelling that sometimes no transformation will occur. This is not necessarily a personal defect of yours. This may be, instead, the nature of your high calling: when you blow the trumpet, it may happen that no one will be ready to answer.

The hope of this book is that you will be able to combine the knowledge of how to work toward transformation with the patience to let it happen out of your control. You will understand pieces that contribute to transformation, while understanding that they form a whole greater than the sum of their parts. You will have manageable steps to take that will improve your storytelling, while acknowledging the periodic need to change the path, dance backwards, or leap into the unknown.

When transformation fails to appear, you will return to your garden. Like any experienced gardener, you will have ideas of what to try next time—and no certainty about what will work. And when transformation does come, you will welcome it with joy, gratitude, and humility. You will have served, at least for that moment, as an agent for the truing of the world.

APPENDIX:
How to Find Storytelling Organizations and Publications

If you have access to the World Wide Web, visit these two sites for up-to-date listings of storytelling resources, including international, national and regional storytelling organizations:

The Storytelling FAQ:
    http://www.lilliput.co.uk

Norwegian Association of Storytelling:
    http://home.newmedia.no/~nff/nffenglish.html

The author of this book maintains web pages with articles, upcoming events, and links to other sites, as well as up-to-date information about storytelling email lists:
    http://www.storyvision.com
    http://www.embolding.com

The best single way to get connected to the world of storytelling is to join the (soon to be renamed) National Storytelling Membership Association. Members receive a magazine, *Storytelling*, and various annual publications. NSMA sponsors the National Storytelling Conference and co-sponsors the National Storytelling

Festival, as well as selling books, videos, and audiotapes via its *Catalog of Storytelling Resources* and *The National Storytelling Press*. Its web site offers discussion boards along with information about NSMA and storytelling in general. NSMA's mission is the nurturing of the community of storytellers.

National Storytelling Membership Association
116½ West Main Street, Jonesborough, TN 37659
800–525–4514 or 615-753-2171
http://www.storynet.org

NSMA's sister organization, Storytelling Foundation, International, produces and co-sponsors the National Storytelling Festival in Jonesborough, TN, and runs the National Storytelling Center, including the library and archives of the first years of the storytelling revival in the United States. SFI's mission includes conducting projects that offer visibility for storytelling, such as its *Storytelling and Leadership* program. SFI does not accept memberships, but you may become a donor in support of its work.

Storytelling Foundation, International
116 West Main Street, Jonesborough, TN 37659
423–753–2171 or 800–952–8392

An excellent survey of books, publishers, and other storytelling resources appears in Holt and Mooney (see bibliography).

NOTES

All references are to entries in the Bibliography.

INTRODUCTION: STORYTELLING BASICS AND BEYOND

Page 13: The idea of the "bad second performance" comes from Barker.

CHAPTER 1: ORAL LANGUAGE

Page 26: For an essay about (and a photo of) the African and African-American gesture of "sucking teeth," see Rickford and Rickford.

Page 28: African-American and European-American expectations about eye contact are contrasted on page 96 of Scheflen.

Page 37: The idea of oral repetition producing an effect similar to ritual appears in Lüthi, *The European Folktale*, 46 and following.

Page 38: The "Law of Two to a Scene" is laid out in Olrik.

CHAPTER 2: FORMS OF IMAGERY

Page 44: For more on the historical shifts in sensory imagery, see Classen.

Page 46: The current name and address of the national Kodály center is Kodály Institute at Capitol, Conservatory of Music, Capitol University, Columbus OH 43209-2394. They have materials on Kodály-inspired music education and can put you in touch with the various organizations of Kodály music teachers. A brief history of the Kodály approach to music education can be heard on Lipman, *Grass Roots*.

CHAPTER 3: IMAGINING FULLY

Page 47: The opening of the Grimms' "Snow White" is from Lang.

Page 49: The exercise of imagining ink drops is inspired by de Mille.

Page 51: Musician Stan Strickland first called my attention to the complex sounds within a sound.

Page 55: The Jewish mystical story can be heard on my *The Soul of Hope*. The rehearsal buddy who asked me what the universal voice sounded like was Sandra Miller.

CHAPTER 4: KINESTHETIC IMAGERY AND CHARACTERIZATION

Page 57: A discussion of "internal tone" appears in Kagan, 285-90.

Page 58: My recording of "The Chicken Woman" can be heard on *Folktales of Strong Women*.

Page 63: The process of developing habitual muscular tensions (as a way of holding in emotions) can be reversed. See also the section on Emotional Blocks in Lipman, *Storytelling Coach*, 157.

Page 65: The story told by the villain, "Pulling the Thorn," is recorded on Lipman, *Forgotten*.

Page 66: For the Chekhov technique, see *On the Technique of Acting*.

Page 67: For background on "The Satan" in Hebrew, Christian, and other traditions, see Forsyth and Pagels.

Page 68: My rehearsal buddy for my work on The Adversary's physical stance was Deborah Gordon Zaslow.

CHAPTER 5: WHAT IS A STORY?

Page 75: The study of school children is described in Romaine, 197–99.

Page 75: The Balinese lack of expectation that a story will be related in chronological order is mentioned in Bateson, 114.

Page 76: The qualities of fairy-tale style are described in works by Swiss folklorist Max Lüthi, *Once* and *European*.

CHAPTER 6: LEARNING THE STORY

Page 81: The obstacles to learning and telling stories are treated in Lipman, *Storytelling Coach*.

CHAPTER 7: DISCOVERING THE MEANING

Page 92: Maud Long's version of "Jack and the Bull" can be heard on Long. I recorded my version on *Milk from the Bull's Horn*.

Page 93: The preference among Eastern European Jews for stories with morals is discussed in Kirshenblatt-Gimblett.

CHAPTER 9: MEMORIZING

Page 101: A discussion of "word-for-word" memorization in oral cultures can be found in pages 57–68 of Ong.

Page 103: "Jack and the Beanstalk" is known to folklorists as Type 328. The best-known version is in Jacobs; and an early printed one, as well as a brief history of the story, appears in Opie and Opie.

SECTION 3: YOUR RELATIONSHIP TO YOUR LISTENERS

Page 111: For a discussion of the listener as helper, see Lipman, *Storytelling Coach* (especially 225–30) and the video *Coaching Storytellers*.

CHAPTER 10: HELPER AND BENEFICIARY

Page 121: The story of Zusia is printed in Lipman, *Storytelling Coach*, 31. It's recorded on Lipman, *Forgotten Story* and *A Storytelling Treasury*.

Page 122: Labov's observation about personal stories is on page 366 of *Language of the Inner City*.

Page 123: I discuss listening on pages 48–54 of *Storytelling Coach*.

Page 124: For more on reminding yourself about "the current reality" as a way of dealing with feelings, see Lipman, *Storytelling Coach*, 166–74.

CHAPTER 11: THE FOUR TASKS

Page 131: For an inspirational description by Laura Simms of telling to the one eager listener in a crowd (which was called to my attention by Laura Beasley), see Holt and Mooney, 95-99.

Page 133: For a coaching session with a storyteller who continued to "invite" after the audience had accepted, see Pauline's session on pages 144–45 of Lipman, *Storytelling Coach*.

Page 133: Trying to gain too much response to your invitation can be a form of "misdirected effort," which is dealt with at length in Lipman, *Storytelling Coach*, 137–56.

Page 134: My "feelings buddy" who helped me with my feelings toward the audience (in "The Soul of Hope") was Jane Winans.

CHAPTER 12: YOUR EFFECT ON YOUR LISTENERS

Page 138: For more on the trance state, see Stallings.

Page 140: Julie Meltzer wrote her master's thesis (at Lesley College, Cambridge, Massachusetts) comparing the story listening response to a shamanic journey.

Page 140: For a coaching session with a storyteller who learns to trust his audience's "leaning back" response, see Lipman, *Storytelling Coach*, 181–87, and Steve's session on the video *Coaching Storytellers*.

CHAPTER 13: PROGRAM PLANNING

Page 147: For an introduction to Hasidism and the Baal Shem Tov, read Wiesel. Some Hasidic stories and a bibliography of Hasidic stories are included on Lipman, *Forgotten Story*. On the World Wide Web, go to http://www.storyvision.com/hasidic

A version of the story I was "called" to tell about the old woman and the Baal Shem Tov appears in Buber as "The Soul Which Descended."

CHAPTER 14: DEVELOPING AUDIENCES FOR YOUR NEEDS

Page 149: The role of the rehearsal buddy (and, of course, of the coach in general) is discussed in Lipman, *Storytelling Coach,* especially 224–37.

Page 151: The traditional stories about the male role are recorded on Lipman, *Milk from the Bull's Horn.*

CHAPTER 15: YOUR VOICE

For more on vocal relaxation techniques, see McClosky.

Page 158: Marsha Saxton told me of her experience getting a patient to yawn when she was a speech pathologist.

Page 163: For cultural preferences regarding vocal quality, see Lomax.

Page 164: My voice teacher, Derek Burrows, is not responsible for my interpretations of the exercises he has given me; but I am grateful for what he has taught, much of which is included in this chapter. Derek is also a storyteller and musician who gives workshops and performances: Derek Burrows, 2 Glenvale Terrace, Jamaica Plain, MA 02130, (617) 983-9184 (derekbur@aol.com, www.derekburrows.com).

CHAPTER 16: PERFORMANCE ANXIETY

Another description of the emotional healing process (from the point of view of listening skills for parents) is in a series of booklets (available in English and in Spanish) by Patty Wipfler (Parents Leadership Institute, P.O. Box 50492, Palo Alto, CA 94303).

Page 174: "The Chicken Woman" is on my recording *Folktales of Strong Women.*

Page 179: Jay O'Callahan's story "Glasses" can be heard on *Coming Home to Someplace New.*

CHAPTER 17: YOUR SUPPORT TEAM

Page 181: A detailed description of the role of the "planning buddy" is on the World Wide Web at http://www.storyvision.com.

SECTION 5: PUTTING IT ALL TOGETHER

Carrie van der Laan, Pam McGrath, and Fran Yardley all helped me articulate the main point of this section.

CHAPTER 18: THE FLEXIBLE SHIFTING OF ATTENTION

Page 195: With regard to the problem of trying *not* to think of something, refer to "Misdirected Effort," in Lipman, *Storytelling Coach,* 137–56.

CHAPTER 19: BALANCING THE DETAILS WITH THE GOALS

Page 201: The scene in which the hero finds his friend dead can be heard in the first act of my *The Soul of Hope.*

BIBLIOGRAPHY

A Storytelling Treasury: Live from the 20th National Storytelling Festival. Jonesborough, TN: National Storytelling Press, 1993. Five audiotapes.

Barker, Clive. *Theatre Games*. London: Methuen, 1992 (1977).

Bateson, Gregory. "Bali: the Value System of a Steady State." *In Steps to an Ecology of Mind*, 107–127. New York: Ballantine Books, 1972.

Buber, Martin. *The Legend of the Baal-Shem*. New York: Schocken Books, 1969.

Chekhov, Michael. *On the Technique of Acting*. New York: Harper Perennial, 1991.

Classen, Constance. *Worlds of Sense: Exploring the Senses in History and Across Cultures*. New York: Routledge, 1993.

de Mille, Richard. *Put Your Mother on the Ceiling: Children's Imagination Games*. New York: Walker and Company, 1967.

Forsyth, Neil. *The Old Enemy: Satan and the Combat Myth*. Princeton, NJ: Princeton University Press, 1987.

Hicks, Ray. *Telling Four Traditional "Jack Tales."* Sharon, CT: Folk-Legacy Records, 1964. FTA-14. Long-playing record.

Holt, David, and Bill Mooney, eds. *Ready-To-Tell Tales: Sure-Fire Stories from America's Favorite Storytellers*. Little Rock: August House, 1994.

Jacobs, Joseph, coll. *English Fairy Tales*. New York: Schocken Books, 1967.

Kagan, Jerome. *Galen's Prophecy: Temperament in Human Nature*. New York: Basic Books, 1994.

Kirshenblatt-Gimblett, Barbara. "The Concept and Varieties of Narrative Performance in East European Jewish Culture." In *Explorations in the Ethnography of Speaking*, edited by Richard

Bauman and Joel Sherzer, 283–308. 2d ed. New York: Cambridge University Press, 1991.

Labov, William. *Language in the Inner City: Studies in the Black English Vernacular.* Philadelphia: University of Pennsylvania Press, 1972.

Lang, Andrew, ed. *The Red Fairy Book.* 1890. Reprint, New York: Dover Publications, 1966.

Lipman, Doug. *Coaching Storytellers: A Demonstration Workshop for All Who Use Oral Communication.* Somerville, MA: Enchanters Press, 1993. Videotape, 81 minutes.

———. *Folktales of Strong Women.* Cambridge, MA: Yellow Moon Press, 1984. Audiotape.

———. *The Forgotten Story: Tales of Wise Jewish Men.* Cambridge, MA: Yellow Moon Press, 1988. Audiotape.

———. *Grass Roots and Mountain Peaks: Taking Charge of Our Future.* Audio recording of keynote speech, Simmons College, Boston MA. Somerville MA: Enchanters Press, 1993. Audiotape.

———. *Milk from the Bull's Horn: Tales of Nurturing Men.* Cambridge, MA: Yellow Moon Press, 1986. Audiotape.

———. *The Soul of Hope: A Jewish Mystical Adventure.* Somerville, MA: Enchanters Press, 1998. Two audiotapes.

———. *The Storytelling Coach: How to Listen, Praise, and Bring Out People's Best.* Little Rock: August House, 1995.

Lipman, Paul, and Doug Lipman. "Such Things to Write About" In *Many Voices: True Tales from America's Past,* edited by Mary C. Weaver, 166–73. Jonesborough, TN: National Storytelling Press, 1995.

Lomax, Alan. *Folk Song Style and Culture.* Washington, DC: American Association for the Advancement of Science, 1968.

Long, Maud. *Jack Tales: Told by Mrs. Maud Long of Hot Springs, North Carolina, 1947.* Vol. 1. Recorded Sound Section, Music Division, Library of Congress, Washington, DC 20540. AFS L47. Long-playing record.

Lüthi, Max. *Once Upon a Time: On the Nature of Fairy Tales.* Bloomington IN: Indiana University Press, 1976.

———. *The European Folktale: Form and Nature.* Philadelphia: Institute for the Study of Human Issues, 1982.

McClosky, David Blair, and Barbara H. McClosky. *Voice in Song and Speech.* Boston: Boston Music, 1984.

Mooney, Bill, and David Holt. *The Storyteller's Guide: Storytellers Share Advice for the Classroom, Boardroom, Showroom, Podium, Pulpit and Center Stage.* Little Rock: August House, 1996.

O'Callahan, Jay. *Coming Home to Someplace New: the Pill Hill Stories.* Marshfield, MA: Artana Publications, 1990. Two audiotapes.

Olrik, Axel, "Epic Laws of Folk Narrative." In *The Study of Folklore,* edited by Alan Dundes, 129–41. Englewood Cliffs, NJ: Prentice-Hall, 1965.

Ong, Walter J. *Orality and Literacy: The Technologizing of the Word.* New York: Routledge, 1982.

Opie, Iona, and Peter Opie. *The Classic Fairy Tales.* London: Oxford University Press, 1974.

Pagels, Elaine. *The Origin of Satan.* New York: Vintage Books, 1995.

Rickford, John A., and Angela E. Rickford. "Cut Eye and Suck Teeth: African Words and Gestures in New World Guise." In *Readings in American Folklore,* edited by Jan Harold Brunvand, New York: W.W. Norton, 1979.

Romaine, Suzanne. *Language in Society: An Introduction to Sociolinguistics.* New York: Oxford University Press, 1994.

Scheflen, Albert E. *Body Language and Social Order: Communication as Behavioral Control.* Englewood Cliffs, NJ: Prentice-Hall, Inc., 1972.

Stallings, Fran. "The Web of Silence: Storytelling's Power to Hypnotize." *National Storytelling Journal.* Spring/Summer 1988: 6–19.

Wiesel, Elie. *Souls on Fire: Portraits and Legends of Hasidic Masters.* New York: Random House, 1972.